# THE PASTOR'S CAT

# THE

# *Pastor's Cat*

# AND OTHER PEOPLE

By
EDWARD VINCENT DAILEY

*Illustrations by* EDWARD F. JOHNSON

*Cat Sketches by* "SHEP"

THE BRUCE PUBLISHING COMPANY
MILWAUKEE

Nihil obstat:

    JOHN A. SCHULIEN, S.T.D.
    *Censor librorum*

Imprimatur:

    ✠ ALBERT G. MEYER
    *Archiepiscopus Milwauchiensis*

    11a Augusti, 1955

Rosary College Dewey Classification Number: 920

Library of Congress Catalog Card Number: 55–11515

TO THE MEMORY OF MY MOTHER

# Foreword

By CLEM LANE, city editor, *Chicago Daily News*

Background for this book is Holy Name Cathedral parish in Chicago. The parish lies just north of Chicago's downtown district, more familiarly, The Loop. The parish is a neighborhood of extremes, a neighborhood of sharp, often violent contrasts.

East of the Cathedral lies the Gold Coast, where wealth and society live in luxurious homes and apartments. Here rise hotels by the dozen, among them the world famous Drake. Here is that street of shops and buildings that has been named The Magnificent Mile. Here is the downtown campus of Northwestern University, its buildings stretching in handsome solidarity for several blocks. And Loyola University's downtown schools, housed in a skyscraper. And here, too, are some of the nation's finest hospitals. And the more fashionable churches of our separated brethren.

Not far from the Cathedral is a frowzy Skid Row. And almost within its shadow are night clubs, clip joints, and roughneck saloons where anything might happen. And frequently does. Handbooks flourish.

Civic organizations charge that these spots are controlled by "The Syndicate," that shadowy organization of racketeers which fell heir to the underworld power held in prohibition days by Al Capone and his gang.

Here within these few square miles one finds all the races of man, black and brown and yellow and white. Some of the worst representatives of these races. And some of the best.

Not too far from the Gold Coast and The Magnificent Mile are slums, alive with rats, crawling with vermin; tired old buildings where sanitary laws and decent codes are mocked. Poverty, clean, is no disgrace; poverty where cleanliness is almost an impossibility, where privacy is a lost cause, is a degrading thing. And it's that kind of poverty in these slums.

In the heart of the district is the Chicago Avenue Police Station, scene of one of this book's fine chapters. Some policemen have left their tour of duty there with fattened bank accounts. For others, the district has meant sleepless nights, frustration, heartbreak. There seems no middle way.

Vice is here in all its forms, all its deformities. But here, too, is Holy Name Cathedral, a rock and a refuge; and a spring whence flows the grace of God. Inevitably there comes to mind St. Paul's striking: "And where sin abounded, grace did more abound" (Rom. 5:20).

Msgr. Dailey has given us twenty-one stories, most of them with a happy ending. Mystery stories, they could be called, for they deal with the action of God's grace in the mysterious, never-to-be-foreseen fashion in which God is wont to operate.

Although we have a book here that is peculiarly Chicago, stories about Chicago men and Chicago women, we have at the same time a book with a theme, a message so universal, so catholic, as to make time and place and names mere accidentals.

The stories in this book are all rooted in reality. Most of the characters I, as a newspaperman, knew, some of them intimately. For their appearance here, they haven't had their noses powdered or their cheeks rouged. Msgr. Dailey has taken them as he saw them and knew them and has set down their stories. Not, on occasion, without a sense of awe, a touch of humility.

Msgr. Dailey has been a priest for twenty-five years. He is now pastor of St. Veronica's church on Chicago's northwest side. But for many years of his priesthood, he lived and worked in Holy Name parish, first as a curate, later as editor of *The New World*, official weekly of the Chicago archdiocese.

His has been an active ministry. He has served as director of the Cathedral Open Forum, often made lively when the summertime orators of Bughouse Square came to joust with their Catholic neighbors; director of the Catholic Fellowship Club of Northwestern University's downtown campus; chaplain (and co-founder with Msgr. Joseph Morrison, former Cathedral rector) of the Catholic Lawyers' Guild; chaplain of the Catholic Actors' Guild, and director of Maryhouse, haven for homeless women in the depths of the Depression.

Msgr. Dailey has brought to this book the knowledge and experience gained in this active life. He has brought, too, a quiet humor, the observant eye and the alert ear of the veteran newspaperman. Above all there shines forth from this book the charity of a good priest.

I can picture a heckler asserting that the author has limited his stories to the lives of unusual persons. But doesn't anyone touched by God's grace become a "new man," a different person, an exciting person, a person worth hearing about?

As for the pastor's cat — there are hunting dogs called pointers for an obvious reason. Could be that this is the first cat so employed?

# $\mathcal{P}$retrial

HE GLARES through his whiskers. His head is battered but erect. The evidence is damning; the marks of his meanderings are proof patent of his guilt. A dirty bandage presses down his left ear; the other points out at an angry angle. One paw is twice the size of the other. His back is a taut arch of defiance.

Judgments on cats are weighed in different scales from those in the courts of men. They are just cats and not men, although they act a lot like men at times.

I may seem a biased judge; but this cat's exploits are

beyond the pale of clemency. He has condemned himself. I see no hope for him; not so much because my feelings against the feline race are so intense, but because of that unconverted noiseless glare of his.

I try to gavel down his incivility. Now it seems to soften into a querulous green or gray, as if he wished that I could understand.

And I begin to think.

# Contents

# THE PASTOR'S CAT

# The Bookkeeper

AS A young man I was always amazed by the inexhaustible mercy of Christ. I had waded knee-deep through scriptural truths and the doctrinal arguments presented in the New Testament. And there came a feeling of intellectual contentment with Calvary, the foundation of the Church, the sacraments, and the many other convincing proofs which underlie Christian teaching.

The over-all commiseration of Christ for the lost sheep seemed overwhelmingly logical, because it was a primary reason for His coming to earth. "I am not come to call the just, but the sinners."

3

Christ would be solicitous for the sick of soul. He was the Physician coming not to heal the well. He was the Good Samaritan coming to drag out of the ditch the ones whom society would pass by with disdain. He wrote in the sand around the woman caught in sin by the hypocrites, who dared not cross the line, as they themselves were not "without sin." He threw His divine weight against the carping Pharisees because of the Magdalen, who washed His feet with tears and dried them with her tumbling, troubled hair; and wherever the Gospel would be preached her name would be remembered.

Perhaps a young priest is most inspired by this positive action of Christ toward all those who are broken in soul or in body; and as his people start crowding into the confessional, the rectory, and bumping into him on the street corner, there comes a feeling that the romance of grace and forgiveness is always working through the unpredictable avenues of Christ's love, that He uses the instruments of persons, places, and circumstance for His planned conspiracy to bring all men to Him.

So after twenty-five years of instrumentation, I have come to realize the values in St. Paul's statement, "Oh the depth of the riches of the wisdom and of the knowledge of God! How incomprehensible are His judgments, and how unsearchable His ways!"

I have noticed also among sinners that there is a sort of spiritual plot which is aimed in the general direction of stealing just a little bit of heaven. Strangely enough their accomplice is Christ, who dragged the Good Thief from the gnarled wood of the cross to the sweetness of unending glory.

A person who has struggled back to God usually cannot contain his happiness. He will contact another straying sheep:

"It's not so bad," he might say.

"You're not going to live forever — why don't you get yourself organized?"

"The priest will understand."

"If you get yourself back you'll be surprised what it will do for your peace of mind."

"Psychiatrist?"

"Quit fooling yourself."

"All you need is enough courage to make a clean breast of it."

"Get in where you belong!"

This grapevine of suggestion starts a parade of people who are urged on by erstwhile sinners who now feel the joy of a cleaner, better life. For some indefinable reason I have found, in a neighborhood notorious for vice, that the foment of grace in the gutter so often brought those who passed by into the blessed company of Mary from Magdala.

I could have called these portraits "God's My Bookkeeper." Many of them concern mine-run folk whom certain social arbitrators would look upon with condescending pity, others with the heartless glare of those who heard the thunder of that challenge: "He who is without sin let him cast the first stone."

Naturally, people who become squared around with God can feel quite content in the dragnet of His grace. It makes no great difference in the end what other people think. They may never measure up to the demands of those who constitute themselves the last word in matters of life and death.

Recording angels and celestial stenographers must be kept quite busy and they must become greatly disturbed by these goings on below. So God must keep the accounts and, most important, balance off the books.

This proposition is very important to all of us. First of all it enables us to understand many of our friends who somehow or other do not have the gift of faith in the theological sense of the word. Second, it consoles us personally that the God of Justice and Mercy will be our final judge. If the verdict of an earthly court or the purblind opinion of people constituted the final stamp of approval upon our lives, I'm afraid the cards would be stacked against us.

God, as the Eternal Bookkeeper, understands why we can so easily lurch into the red; because He made us, He realizes what blundering mistakes we can make, how badly we can mix up our credits and debits.

But no matter how poorly we conduct the business of our soul, we are never thrust into bankruptcy, a receivership is never declared over our spiritual estate; instead of throwing the book at us at the end, He throws it away — if we so much as reach for His hand in penitence and love.

So it is, when the great hush of night cloaks the city and our thoughts find focus in the backdrop of reality, we are consoled with what we all know — that, after all, God is our Bookkeeper.

# The Cat

THE PASTOR'S CAT enters properly enough.

He was so much like human beings in his perversity. With the skill of a trained demolitionist, he frequently threatened to disrupt parish organization.

Our organist is a woman of patience, which in itself is rather extraordinary. Many organists are notoriously short tempered; and when the cat felt like dashing over the pedal tones during a High Mass, there were passing flurries of anger. The crisis came when the cat actually pressed his front paws on the treble clef during a requiem. Even our long suffering musician could not countenance this stab at an aria from Mozart.

But these tendencies to take over a man's or a woman's

job is not why the cat deserves top billing in these pages. He, after all, symbolizes a "stray," one who would continue to venture into his world of alley fights which returned him more often the loser; but he is like people and his contribution was great and in the end he landed on his feet.

So the feline who converted no one but the parish priest, did earn his laurels, doubtful as they might be. Although very little can be written about a cat's mind, this one's behavior was as provocative as the old gimmick about the mouse playing the baby grand. His abilities were not just limited to mice. He took part in ceremonies, in the conduct of parish meetings, used his fur as a duster for the pews, and nearly had the statue of St. Anthony beating a retreat from his scratching efforts to climb into the Saint's arms.

I have a faint recollection that at one time a cat bit me and that the neighborhood boys got together and decided that the only manly animal habits were possessed by the dog, preferably a mastiff with sinews of steel. Perhaps the lap cat type revolted a youngster whose enthusiasm ran to the football field or the basketball court. The picture of a Siamese lolling uselessly around just didn't fit in with the positive action program of a young American.

I reached manhood with a dislike for cats. I would sooner have owned a hyena than a highbred Maltese. During the years as an editor, I scarcely thought of cats or their place in society; but an appointment to a parish in the city changed all this in a hurry.

Ordinarily a new pastor feels his way rather slowly.

He tries to find out about the problems, the various societies, the projects to be encouraged, the capabilities of the fine people who come under his jurisdiction. Usually they soft-pedal grave difficulties for a while in the hope that the new pastor will stumble over them himself.

For me the routine work went forward without a hitch. Then one day a delegation appeared.

"It's about your cat, Father."

I knew I had a boiler which shot off steam with undisciplined fury. I knew I had foundation erosion which necessitated lowering the rectory three inches. I knew I had difficulties with sump pumps, tuck-pointing, electricity, and heat. I knew that the great void in my education was not to have taken a complete course in engineering.

But I didn't know I had a cat!

And of course I couldn't know that the beast would cause me more trouble than all the mechanical breakdowns combined. It seems to me that he just walked into the boiler room one cold night and took over. If he had been a perfect cat, he would have confined his maneuvers to mice in the back of the church; but he had what a psychiatrist might call a "compulsion neurosis." He would tear down the aisles for no good reason. Men and women attending services became quite used to feeling a fast swish across their ankles as they knelt in prayer. All except the delegation.

"Father, the cat should be thrown out. He lies down on the sanctuary carpets. He glares back at us. He stands guard over the vigil-light stand. We would like to have a candle once in a while. He prowls up and down the aisles like he owns the place. How can you stand it?"

There seemed only one course to take. Good will was important. But the cat stayed simply because he had a singularity of purpose which most of the members of the delegation did not have. In spite of his seemingly irrelevant actions, he was dedicated to the extermination of rodents.

During the rat-mouse epidemic, when the city talked of laws about the menace, there were few to be found on the church or school properties. I soon realized that the reason I didn't know I had a cat was that he was too busy on his unappointed mission to bother about calling on me.

When the tempers of a few of the members of the delegation were just about cooled down, my hand was nearly forced against my undercover agent.

Weddings are always supposed to go smoothly. Rehearsals are held. The bride and groom are naturally in a high state of excitement. They want to look good in a ceremony which usually occurs once in their lifetime.

This particular nuptial was one of our best. Most of our parishioners were present and everyone agreed that the church looked beautiful and the bride out of this world. The doors were closed against the noises of the street, all except the one which led to the boiler room, where three mechanics were in a heated argument about pipes and return valves. Either the cat became frightened or resentful. Quick as a wink he plunged across the sanctuary, over and around the trailing gown of the frightened bride who had just gotten out the words, "I will." Then, perched on the seat where the priest often sits during ceremonies, he watched the proceedings, apparently not caring that judgment would soon be pronounced on his unliturgical activities.

Despite provocations, the cat's absolute banishment seemed out of the question, because I had come to a sickening realization that he had become nonexpendable. The traps and the other devices I had hoped to substitute just couldn't move around after their prey. They could not telegraph that "this is not for us," a message which mice seem to get when a place is so expertly covered by their natural adversary.

But Christmas time brought a major crisis. A demure little nun had taken charge of decorating the crib in the sanctuary. She was usually most helpful, precise, and possessed of a sufficient degree of humility. This last virtue apparently did not encompass my now notorious cat. She could not be persuaded that there was any good whatsoever in this particular "stray." He was the bête noire of her usually tranquil existence.

As the figures of the magi, the donkey, the sheep, the cattle were lined up in proper order, she, like most nuns, began to gather enthusiasm at the prospect of a Midnight Mass. She looked forward to the nostalgic silence, the choir, the beautiful crib; and of course to the placing of the statue of the Infant Jesus just before Mass would begin. She was content. Her fatigue gave way to joy as she made her way to the convent. Never had things worked out so well!

Just as darkness settled over the white, quiet earth, a clamor came from a crowd of boys who were in and out of the church that night.

"Father, hurry up! The crib! Sister, look what happened!"

Thoughts of fire, calamity — everything — raced through my mind. Just a glance, settled and unsettled the whole issue.

Beneath the Blessed Virgin's altar was the Christmas grotto in all its splendor. Lights played gently on the little crib filled with straw. Angels looked down in great wonder.

The Infant Jesus was not there! He just couldn't get in. The cat lay contentedly in the warm hollows of the straw, with great eyes peering at the excited children, who considered the whole episode a paralyzing high point in parish melodrama.

The Sister, usually so composed and charitable, just said, "That creature!" putting into the phrase all the disgust and disappointment at her command.

There was only one explanation for me to give. I was caught in the middle and I thought I saw St. Anthony smile a little as I said:

"After all, children, God loved animals from all eternity. He wanted them to be around His divine Son's birth. The cat is a live representative of the donkey, the cattle, the sheep which comforted Him that night. He has to have his Christmas. He is just warming up the straw for Christ — Sister, please bring in the statue now."

Happily no further argument was needed.

There had been nights when I lay awake wondering how I could keep the big mischievous intruder under control. I had dreamed of his tearing through doors in a flurry of bristling whiskers and legs.

But that was all over. The pastor's cat solved it all in one fast jump into the crib on Christmas Eve. He became a hero to the children. Unquestionably he was here to stay.

And I even think he knows I don't like cats.

# Maryhouse

THE antics of grace operating on city streets should not be surprising. Christ walked the streets of Jerusalem and gently brushed the multitudes with the touch of His mercy and forgiveness. The largess of His grace was not confined to the synagogue or to the established places of worship. There were, and always will be, other avenues for His influence.

For instance, there was Maryhouse.

There were people who entered it, people who lived in it, people who just helped. Always they were examples of how the fingers of God juggled their destinies.

It was the winter of 1935. Ordinarily one winter is about the same as another in Chicago: sudden storms, severe cold, gloomy days, bitter nights, cars stalled, traffic jammed; sunny days, thaws, freeze-ups again.

The year 1935 was different. Over the huge drifts of snow and ice, came the backwash of the great depression. After the World's Fair, many young and older women found themselves unemployed. They had nothing to do and nowhere to go.

A great number of these went to live in the 42nd Ward on the Near North Side. They had been the same as any other persons to begin with; but they soon became a part of a place which was different from any other on earth. The people and the events which flecked around them were a kaleidoscope, where every emotion, every sin, every virtue, tumbled around in unique lights and darks.

Standing in solid vigilance over the neighborhood, is the Holy Name Cathedral, to which I had been assigned as an assistant pastor. The massive stone structure seemed to symbolize strength in a little world which offered little hope.

Naturally the problems of the wanderers became ours. We who assisted in the duties of a parish so various in its demands, were strained no end to meet the poverty and the vice which sprawled so prodigally to the south and west along the honky-tonk, saloon-jammed, sin-sodden streets.

One stormy night an idea was born in a restaurant at Halsted and Randolph streets, in the very hub of Chicago's great produce market. There Barney Kessell reigned with absolute power. He couldn't forget the dreary years of childhood when he sold papers on 12th Street, the striving for success in small eating places, where a stein of beer entitled the customer to a meal; then the days, when broke and discouraged, he established the now famous Barney's Market Club, which featured the biggest and the best in steaks, lobster, and chops.

There was nothing small about Barney, either. He was a squat, rotund person who could have easily posed for the figure of the typical proprietor on the murals which surrounded his place. His capacious waist was always encircled by an apron. With sleeves rolled up, his old-fashioned shoes laced over white stockinged feet, he kept his luminous, twinkle-shot brown eyes always glued on the droves of incoming customers, as if he feared that some day they would stop coming in. He never quite understood how things could be so good.

He could seldom remember names; and his "Yes sir, Senator — how many?" was the watchword of this wondrous spot of fine eating and good cheer.

Money poured in. The restaurant was enlarged. Two more rooms were built to accommodate the crowds, as nationwide publicity brought in conventioneers by the thousands, gourmets, and just plain, hungry people. But Barney never forgot the dismal time of his own hunger, the creditors clamoring at his door, the discouragement of trying to find friends when his fortunes had fled.

We were sitting before one of his mammoth steaks. The many other good things to eat seemed too plentiful. Barney braced his chubby elbows on the table as he talked. We got around to the jobless who groped through the streets nearby, how they would build fires beneath the bridge to keep from freezing to death, how they shook so frightfully in the grip of despair and the pains of an empty stomach.

It was agreed that if I could lease a hotel he would do the rest. Fortunately there was an understanding rector at the Cathedral. Monsignor Morrison lent a sympathetic ear. He knew the wretched conditions in the west end of his parish and that the main burden rested on his shoulders. He would allow forty dollars a month from the treasury. Although the whole thing seemed a little on the "wild-cat" side, the Monsignor had faith in any venture which touched upon grace.

After that we were on our own.

A yellow, weary looking hotel at 607 N. Wells Street was chosen for the experiment. Strategically, it was in the very heart of the Near North Side. "Maryhouse" became its name. For several years it accomplished much in a field where loveless government efforts often fail.

Barney Kessell was the heart and the stomach of the institution. He had some money now. Much of it went for brand new beds, linoleum, and truck loads of food. Hungry women found Maryhouse a haven from the harsh, unsympathetic streets. Morals-court cases began to realize that hope could be found in the house which asked no questions and paid no attention to police records.

Obviously Maryhouse would have quickly become an old folks home if the guests were not shuttled through into worth-while occupations. So the employment bureau became second in importance only to the kitchen. With the co-operation of "people with connections," some 600 jobs were filled with the alumnae of Maryhouse.

In the meantime, a steady supply of victuals tumbled in from the Market Club. The commission merchants always quailed at the piratical raids of Barney along

Randolph Street; the familiar "Come on, how about giving the fadder a bushel of potatoes, a bag of onions, a basket of corn — anything?"

It wasn't exactly sandbagging; but it came mighty close to coercion, this direct pressure from one of their best customers.

Barney's goodness probably stemmed from gratitude. His heart was solidly good. His experience of having been outside looking in prompted him to immediate charities.

One November day I heard the news from his son-in-law.

"Barney died in his sleep this morning."

My first thought was one of loss, that this robust man was no longer around with his bellowing, "Yes sir, Senator," with his little kindnesses so bluntly expressed, with his princely generosity toward the poor, the orphans, and the sick.

I picked up the newspapers which had so often published his exploits.

"Barney Kessell, owner of Barney's Market Club, died Saturday in his home. Although Jewish, he took an active part in charitable work among Catholic organizations."

This sparse statement concealed a world of benevolence. There were the fiestas which he underwrote and which helped build the seminary at Momence, Illinois. Many American and Mexican boys studied here for the priesthood and were ordained priests in the seminary chapel. These benefits cost him thousands of dollars a year.

There was the waitress with three children who told

me that he gruffly pushed into her pocket the money for long standing hospital bills.

There were the countless many he helped in their sorrows.

I like to imagine Barney bringing his bulk to the gates of Paradise, the Old Testament group watching from afar. Barney, of course, knew from his learned father about Moses, Abraham, Isaac, and the others with whom he shared a chosen blood. The Virgin Mother, Queen of the clergy, smiles upon this friend who aided so many to reach her Son's altars. She watches burly St. Peter as he steps to the gates with a nod.

Quickly, with a twinkle, the Fisherman who couldn't forget the kind of hearty man he was himself, does a sentimental switch.

"Yes sir, Senator," he says.

# Virtue in Strange Settings

THE neighborhood of Maryhouse held few surprises for those who lived there during the middle thirties. Recently Patricia Bronte wrote a series of contrasts about the Near North Side in the Chicago *Tribune*.

"It is a part of town which never goes to sleep," she said. "But it is also creative, gay, devout, desperate, assured, fearless, frightening, and as of this minute certainly the liveliest . . . and most fascinating corral of human beings on the face of the earth."

From this maelstrom of frustration and despair came the guests of the little hotel at 607 N. Wells Street. To attempt their complete portraits would be an impossibility. It would be impossible, too, to give statistics on how many made good. Only God kept the books.

If the metallic standards of society were applied to the individual guests, they would have had little chance for survival. Sin has a peculiar way of not seeming so grim when surrounded by a sufficiently attractive background. Many a worldling, whose life is publicly immoral, gets by surprisingly well if he has social attributes, if he features the best in cocktail parties and entertainment. His friends who are impressed by wealth itself somehow give him a pass. The same sins found in the slums are condemned with unmitigated vigor. Nevertheless, Shalimar and charm, sable coats and penthouses cannot change the essence of sin.

I have come across as great virtue on the back streets of the Near North Side as I have on the Gold Coast, where it is sometimes easier to practice. There are different and compelling temptations when one is starving.

As I ponder upon virtue in strange settings, I think of one of the first guests of Maryhouse. It was Saturday night and especially cold. Occasional penitents drifted to the rear of Holy Name Cathedral, where confessions were in progress. The wild whine of the wind pitched irreverently across the still of the old church. I was happy to finish. As I made my way out of the confessional box, I noticed a thin, anxious girl standing near the door. She apparently had been waiting to talk to a priest.

"Father, I am all set to go to Communion tomorrow. But I have no place to go. I haven't had a thing to eat for two days. I've been a hostess in a South State Street saloon. I had to try to sell drinks to the customers — maybe dance with the stumblebums who blew in from the street."

I asked her what made her come over to the church.

"I felt like a slave. I was sick of the whole business. I saw the spire of the Holy Name and just came in . . . and saw the others going in to confession."

It was as if she had timed her decision economically as well as spiritually. Maryhouse had opened a few days before. The woman in charge was anxious for help. It came tailor made. The girl from State Street joined the staff. Using her charms in a different sort of way, she would stand at the door and greet the guests entering the home with the cross on the door. And over that door was the name of Mary, another girl who once looked for shelter in a pagan world.

Another guest also came with a record — an acrobatic one. She had grown up in the circus. Her natural grace combined with tremendous strength enabled her literally to climb the ladder of success in the first years of her career. She became a star aerialist. Hanging from one arm high above the crowd, she would twist, over and over, with a drum keeping a booming count to her gyrations. Everyone was willing to admit that she was the world's champion at this type of performance. And it is true that her working arm was about three inches longer than her other. This entitled her to some acclaim as one who was willing to sacrifice her symmetry for her profession.

But her bigtop tumbled down one day into the dust of the depression. She went broke with as much of a crash as if she had fallen from her perch on the 280th twist.

The Employment Bureau of Maryhouse was hard pressed to apply her talents to a ground level job. Finally she began to work for a moderately wealthy family as second maid, answering the bells and serving at the table. She did pretty well for a few months. Perhaps her long-armed boardinghouse reach was an asset. Maybe it wasn't. It must have reminded her of a gay life and the plaudits of the crowd. Her temporary grip on the grace of the sacraments began to slip, and she suddenly disappeared. One day she stopped at the rectory. She felt she should report back.

She sat in an open convertible car, a very high-priced one. Two Russian wolfhounds sniffed around on the lustrous upholstery.

"How come all this luxury?" I was disturbed.

"I just got lucky; one of those things."

My questions were half answered; and she drove away into what I thought was oblivion.

About fifteen years passed. Many like her came and went. Some strayed. Many stuck to their hard-earned victories of the spirit.

One night I was preparing a Lenten talk on penance, and was knee-deep in material without one up-to-the-minute application. It came right out of the blue in the shape of an airmail letter. A few paragraphs brought me back to high wires and circus tops. I decided to read the letter as a preamble to my talk on penance.

For a sheer, unabashed analysis of a soul in tempest, I have seen nothing better in writing. The sermon I gave was the best I ever gave on penance, not so much because I didn't write it, but rather that the one who did heard the unrelenting voice of God, knew the bitter plunge into despair, so deeply felt the great intrigue of Christ.

"Dear Father," the letter began. "No doubt you remember how I fell from grace and married. [She had entered a legal marriage outside the Church, which troubled her conscience.]

"I certainly seemed to sink deeper and deeper in the quagmire of sin until all that was left was to throw myself completely on the mercy of God and do a right-about-face. God has been good to me and I know He will continue to be so long as I keep close to Him in His Sacrament of Love.

"This I continue to do daily, and, with each thanksgiving, request that no obstacle will be too great for me to overcome in order to lead me back to Him on the morrow.

"You see I have come to realize I am not so self-sufficient and capable. I have to depend on God entirely to keep me going in the right direction.

"Father, I could go into long details on my life, but that is neither necessary nor interesting. All I will say is God broke my health to make me open up my heart and mind again. I was in a wheel chair for months and, don't get me wrong, Father, I was happy the whole time I was in that motorized pair of legs. I knew it was God working some way for me to get back close to Him again. Excuse the slang, please, but God is the one who stays in there and pitches and works everything out in the end.

"Sincerely,
The Girl on the Trapeze"

# Fragments and Frustration

DONATIONS from sympathetic Chicagoans were very helpful in the support of Maryhouse. But its survival for six years depended mostly on the spirit of the men and women who sacrificed their time and energy to its complex problems.

The first managers were women of splendid zeal, who were willing to spend ten hours a day in receiving guests, providing them with rooms, and overseeing their material demands. They made contacts with doctors, lawyers, and dentists who were willing to receive women who needed help; and they always seemed to need it. The employment center was continually sending them out on jobs. Barney's trucks pulled up almost daily to the rear of 607 N. Wells Street and emptied out vegetables and meats. They had to be carried by the women to the second and third floors, where two kitchens were always cooking away.

Sometimes the more temperamental guests would start an intramural warfare to relieve the boredom of their stay. One night a few of the rougher ones, who had been recommended to Maryhouse by the police, threw the place into an uproar by engaging each other in a donnybrook of hair pulling and fisticuffs. Two squad cars pulled up with their sirens screaming. The female pugilists were soon back at the police station for a "cooling off," and quiet was restored for a while.

The first manager lasted only a few weeks, in this revolving world of persons and incident. The new manager was a woman of gentle breeding. She had enough money of her own and time to devote herself exclusively to her ambition: the desire to serve humanity in its lower reaches. Her pleasant manners were seldom ruffled. She succeeded for a time in absorbing the blows of so much social upheaval in the spirit of Christ, which she had in abundance. But three months of it was enough. She began to run down physically, and her mind was tortured with thoughts of failure.

"I can't make it, Father. I can't make it. I'm beaten to a pulp. There is so much to be done. But I haven't the strength or the experience, maybe, to take it day after day. I'm just a sentimental fool, I guess," she finished with a sigh. Her frustration was complete.

I thought of St. Paul's consoling words about "fools for Christ." We could never know how much her gracious foolishness had accomplished in those ninety days.

These managers had a grim enough time of it; but they were provided with lighter moments by some of the casual visitors who came in for a meal or a room for the night. These visitors were harmless wanderers in a section of the city which could fit them in without undue strain. They had highly developed protective instincts, however. They would not be received in the rich suburban areas or the staid neighborhoods to the north, the south, or the west. They felt safe in wandering about the streets close to "Cathedral Square." And they were.

One thin, tense woman asked for help when she needed it. Her background was one of education and culture. She had been a tutor in French, and could always join in a learned conversation on literature and language. She had a slight limp. Many years previously she had fallen from a public conveyance. No one ever knew whether her limp was real or feigned. Some unsympathetic observer said that she still hoped to collect a large insurance settlement and couldn't afford to give up the evidence for her claim.

This observer argued from an incident which occurred during the International Eucharistic Congress in Chicago. A huge crowd was jammed into the Cathedral for a Pontifical Mass. Cardinals, bishops, diplomats, distinguished visitors from countries all over the world were scarcely able to move through the streets, so solidly were they banked with pilgrims.

"Make way for the poor lady," a policeman shouted. A wheel chair slowly rolled through the narrow lane. In it was the French teacher. With tragic appeal in her eyes, she looked straight ahead. As she pushed through the mass of sympathetic people, they were struck with the pathos of the scene.

"She's a dear old person, make room for her," they said when she reached the front steps of the Cathedral. "At least she can get a look through the open door."

For an instant they couldn't believe their eyes. With the vigor of an athlete, she kicked the wheel chair aside, sprinted up the steps and, like a flash, disappeared among the dignitaries inside the church.

Not much was known about the ingenious tutor, except that she loved the companionship of cats and that she was suspicious of people. Fanciful tales were told of her old, dark apartment in an abandoned building near the river front. No one quite believed that she could spend her days contently feeding her pets, and probably conversing with them in high-tone French.

At length she became very ill, and one of the priests in the Cathedral brought her the sacraments.

When he returned he told us that she was dying. "Oh, the cats? Yes — there were 10 or 20 of them jumping in all directions when I opened the door."

After her death she was missed around Maryhouse. In her way, she had amused everyone without harming a soul, not even her own, with her cats, her wheel chair, and her culture.

Another object of neighborhood interest was "Pigeon Jenny," a constant visitor to the same Cathedral Square. She preached an implacable doctrine. To her, feeding pigeons was almost an essential for salvation; and she stood by the hour practicing what she preached. The news of her prodigal feasts soon got around the pigeon kingdom. At times the square was more cluttered than the famous piazza of St. Mark's in Venice.

Occasionally when some priest would get up enough courage to suggest that there were limits even for pigeons, she would follow him along the streets loudly berating him. Her invectives were choice and unforgettable. He would soon realize that having pigeons under foot was much less trouble than having Pigeon Jenny in his ears.

A contemporary of Jenny was an old Irish lady who had saved a good deal of money but who was distrustful of banks. She had her own ambulatory bank, however. It was her six skirts in which she had sewed all of her savings and which she wore day and night. She would sometimes visit friends, but she was hesitant about staying very long anywhere because everyone knew by now where she kept her fortune. And she would be missing a few dollars now and then, if she didn't keep awake and walking about. A policewoman brought her to Maryhouse one day to get her some food and a room.

"Make yourself at home. You can stay here for a while," the policewoman said.

But the Irish lady was never one to linger. She must keep moving all the time, holding on to what she had, with a confused instinct for security. Under the roof she left, there were many who were moved by the same primal instinct of finding security somewhere in that vast jungle outside.

That many of them did more often than not was consolation enough — in spite of the exhausting efforts and the frustration of the managers.

Chances are these fools for Christ offered more than motley and bells to their heavenly King.

# There Were Others

THE subject of Maryhouse and of the neighborhood which absorbed its guests could be explored indefinitely. The original members of the experiment are localized enough. The others who touched on its perimeter have long since broken through into the unknown. How they made out is anyone's guess.

I am sure of this however: Maryhouse became a cross section of that mysterious game of grace which always succeeds in bewildering me. No doubt God calls the plays; and I have often stood on the field, like a safety man in a football game, watching a trick maneuver pile by for a touchdown. Like finger prints, no play seems to be duplicated; and perhaps there are angelic bleachers up yonder from which the cheering Seraphim and Cherubim watch the sinner sprint into the end zone.

For instance there was the dowager, who despite her past opulence and high bred manners, had to eat. The remembrance of her past prestige was greater than her present distress, and prompted her to sidestep the vulgarity of many bread lines. She clung tenaciously to her few clothes and a New England accent while concealing her Maryhouse address. She appeared at study clubs, moved around in better circles, and generally preserved a respected place among the older women of the Near North Side.

However, her calling card was long since buried in her lavender and lace. Her 607 N. Wells was not the Waldorf, although its roof was as sound and the food almost as digestible. With this in mind she circled back to Maryhouse each night until a job could be found for her.

It was not easy to fit her into the right spot. She had high blood pressure and a spent heart. A lady's companion might do. But then she would meet her erstwhile friends who had known her back when.

One day I was surprised to find her at a switchboard in a busy establishment. She was the perfect receptionist. She made one feel like the most important visitor of the day. Courtesy and natural kindness tumbled across the counter.

In a swift descent to reality she said to me,

"Father, don't mention to anyone that I was your guest at Maryhouse."

My reassurance was mingled with flickering signals from the board. When I left, I knew she would never master the intricacies of plugs and little white lights.

I have lost track of this fine old lady who tried to adjust herself to the tempo of our day. But I know she will be happy somewhere along the line. The more earthy ones at Maryhouse remembered the charity of her heart. It was all she could afford. She had long since given large sums to causes of mercy; but I doubt whether a bank note in figures of four could match the effect of her sweetness in a place which needed just that more than anything else.

Maybe we shouldn't worry about the little woman and her smile.

Then there was Sister Mary. She was a receptionist too, having greeted a thousand or more babies into St. Vincent's, Chicago's famous orphan asylum. Many of these babies were from the doorsteps of the rooming houses in Chicago.

The thought of describing her as hundreds of policemen and mothers know her, worries me not a little; because it is hard to evaluate the expanses of a generous soul, especially if you view it against the background of labors which never seek publicity.

But the Daughters of Charity are familiar figures in

reclaiming the sick and orphaned. They have been hero-
ines on battlefields; and they have been just as courageous and merciful in their solicitude to the unwed
mothers. General maternity cases are also handled by
St. Vincent's Hospital, which functions night and day
in watchful solicitude for the poor and unfortunate.

Sister Mary was picked for the front lines because of
her peculiar talents. She was always on hand to receive
the baby in her arms. There are pictures of burly policemen unloading their charges upside down and every
which way into their future home. Tape recordings are
not available of the furious reprimands delivered to the
awkward man on the beat who knew nothing about the
approved method of handling a squirming little waif.
But the hardened officers of the law loved it. They
knew that the tongue lashings they sometimes received
were as false as the tears were true which came into the
eyes of Sister Mary whenever she handled an abandoned
child.

No one was built more like a home than she, very solid,
always good for handouts and a warm welcome. In a
big jolly way, she embodied the spirit of St. Vincent
without realizing it. Her dealings with another side of life
never seemed to tarnish her idealism.

I should regret having unloaded so many vagrants in
her direction; but somehow I justified it by knowing that
they paid for their meals by listening to Sister Mary's
verbal going over of their faults and failures. Even today,
you can test her soft heart by sending anyone to her
for food.

With Maryhouse and St. Vincent's just three blocks

apart, it was inevitable that some working program should be established between them. Before a woman entered St. Vincent's, she would often stay at 607 N. Wells in complete anonymity. Afterward she could face the world with a minimum of embarrassment. There was a constant flow of kitchen supplies, linens, and other staples to Maryhouse from St. Vincent's as a sort of payment.

But my conscience always hurt me. We always received more than we gave. Perhaps the greatest favor of all was a realization of how good so many were who made that three block trip. If they were too bad, they never would have made it.

Sister Mary was present at the blessing of Maryhouse, as was Barney Kessell and the manager of the Congress Hotel. He and his associates contributed iceboxes and stoves, and canned goods for the pantry. Most of the people who appeared that day seemed unsure about the project.

It was worth a glance in all directions: the restaurant man, the nuns, the homeless drifting human beings, looking at Barney, the hardy symbol of food, and at the nun, the just as hearty symbol of the spirit — both willing to work it out on the firm ground of compassion for the soul and the body.

For years there was a little box in the vestibule of the cathedral which, somehow, was always well supplied with money for the maintenance of Maryhouse. I presumed that the regular parishioners were just being kind to us. It never occurred to me that a sizable amount came from other sources, until one day after the depression when I was sitting in the parlor of a well-known dog kennel on East Erie Street.

As usual the place was a bedlam. Pedigreed canines were yowling with that cocksure manner not enjoyed by their country type brethren. People were soothing their little pets as if their social prestige depended on how they controlled their dogs.

After some unimportant conversation, a well-dressed, prosperous looking woman asked for a word with me. Presuming that she sought some advice on training animals, I listened casually until she mentioned Maryhouse.

"Do you remember me?"

I thought for a moment of Lake Shore Drive, of parishioners who lived on the right side of the tracks. Again I was wrong.

"I was a guest at 607 for three months during the depression. I actually contemplated suicide. I was proud, and up to then I had been successful."

Anticipating my curiosity, she came to the point.

"Your employment bureau got me a job. I got the breaks. I am now an executive in a radio corporation."

Naturally this came under the heading of statistics, one of the many which we were able to follow through without effort. We never tried to trace a broken life; but here was one built up again, and with the thought came that peculiar thrill one gets when looking back at work which seemed so futile at the start.

"And, Father," she said, "I never pass the Cathedral without throwing a bill into the box marked 'For Maryhouse.' Maybe other people who are tempted to go east to the Lake will turn around and go west like I did."

Not long ago I pulled my car to the curb on Wells Street and looked over the old hotel. It has slipped badly since those days of Maryhouse. Children were sitting around the door. Many families occupied the floors above. I thought perhaps I should take a picture. Maybe the next time the physical features of the place would be entirely changed or razed.

But then I felt that you just can't get a picture of the spirit any more than you can photograph a radio wave, an electric current, or the stroke of God's grace upon a soul.

The place had served its purpose.

# Morgan Was a Pirate

HELEN MORGAN "reversed the English" on her name-
sake, the renowned buccaneer Henry Morgan, by handing
out to others nearly as much as Henry seized in his piratical raids on the coasts of Central America and the West
Indies in the sixteenth century. She was master of music,
her weapon was a voice, her gold was stolen from a song
and given out with the flourish of a queen. And in the
end, true to form, she plundered her way to the coast of
heaven.

When Helen Morgan died at forty-two, she was making about $4,000 a week, a sum which represented her normal earning power. However, the immortal Helen of "Show Boat" died almost penniless, and her friends and relatives gladly gave her a decent burial. Up to her death she had been on the giving end to an alarming degree.

Helen Morgan had a special talent in entertainment. She would prop up on a piano and sing in a nostalgic way "Just My Bill" or "Only Make Believe," songs which always conjure up her memory. Many an artist could execute them with better tone quality and more volume; but what she had she was able to give out in an inimitable flurry of sentiment and melody.

But Helen was never happy except when she gave out her happiness to others. It seems that the possession of happiness is impossible unless it is being continually handed out. Like anything beautiful, virtue by its nature cannot remain static. It must be on the move. This is especially true of charity, the love of neighbor, the compassionate understanding of another who is down and out.

Helen steps onto the stage of these narratives quite accidentally. In 1935, the Cathedral Guild of Catholic Actors, later The Catholic Actors' Guild of Chicago, was organized at the Holy Name Cathedral to serve the spiritual and temporal needs of those in show business.

Many jobless actors walked the streets with the desperation of those who felt that their names should be flickering on marquees — certainly not on the rolls of relief. Among them were many excellent performers who could have been working six shows a day except for the unemployment obstacles of the early thirties.

Scores of these people roamed about the Near North

Side looking for help. Rooming houses were bulging with nonpaying guests. Maryhouse was available for the actresses, but there was little provision for the men. The Guild decided to run benefits to provide funds for food, shelter, and hospital bills.

We soon discovered that the complex emotional life of the actor concealed a generous, good heart. He might mix himself up badly with the peculiar temptations which would never beset a bridge tender, for instance, or an archaeologist, surrounded by prehistoric dinosaurs. But when called upon to straighten out someone else's life, the showman was generally willing to go all out in his labors.

In a very short time, a host of celebrities gave their services for the upkeep of Maryhouse and especially to the welfare of their down and out companions. A few stalwart supporters come to mind: Fran Allison, an inspiration and leader, June Meredith, Lois Wilson, Ben Bernie, Mitzie Green, Simone Simone, Mary Bryan, Marty May, Joey Faye, Pat Foy, Phillip Lord, Neva Patterson, Pat O'Malley, Skeets Gallagher, Don McNeill, and others.

It was not surprising to find Helen Morgan willing to appear at these benefits whenever possible. For years she had been giving much of her salary to others, anyway.

As I talked to her, it was evident that she had no extraordinary churchgoing record, however extraordinary her charity. No doubt helping to feed the hungry was to her like practicing a sort of faith according to the old formula that charity covers a multitude of things.

Helen Morgan's contributions to the needy were generally unidentified; but her generous spirit no doubt touched on the life of another girl, a dancer in the same theatrical unit, who worshiped the great "Show Boat" star.

This girl was also a talented performer. From her early teens, she knew the admiration of the public, the stage door Johnny, the bouquets at the end of the show. The footlights never seemed to be off in her short, hectic life as a Ziegfield dancer.

The father of this dancer, who was as solemn as the organ notes he pedaled off at various church functions, worried about his daughter in the impractical way of an absorbed musician. But he never quite reached into her conscience, except to question and wonder what would happen if she continued in her lionized role of a charming danseuse.

Then suddenly she was struck down with meningitis. I shall never forget the hurried call and the sight of a one-time healthy girl bent over in twisted torture. Seemingly she had made her last appearance before the public eye.

A priest in an emergency call like this is confronted with peculiar pressures. There is a question of time, and the problem of getting a soul into an attitude of prayer and penance.

In short seconds, he realizes that he is strictly an instrument. Whatever arts of smooth spiritual salesmanship he might possess can be simply derailed in the beginning. The priest is on his own. Armed only with the sacraments, he is in a tempest which only abates when Christ's grace fingers through and touches the other's heart. When it does, it is as definite as His action when He picked up Mary Magdalen that day in the house of Simon the Pharisee.

"Your sins are forgiven — your Faith has saved you. Go in peace."

That night as I left the hospital, I felt that there must be joy in heaven again because of another sinner doing penance. I suppose I labored under the practical conclusion that this was the end. It was better this way. The girl was just twenty years old, and too young to die, according to worldly standards, which frantically strive to vitaminize everyone into dotage. The dancer was in good shape interiorly at least. She was squared off spiritually. She could face the judgment with a passing mark. A return to her old young ways could probably flunk her out in the only examination which really counts.

However, the girl lived, and some time later I paid her a visit. As I made my way to her home, I thought about Francis Thompson, the poet, who had suffered through untold anguish in his struggle with drugs and alcohol. In his "Hound of Heaven" he asked and answered a lot of questions about the ways of God.

"Ah! is Thy love indeed
A weed, albeit an amaranthine weed
Suffering no flowers except its own to mount?
"Ah! must —
"Designer infinite! —
Ah! must Thou char the wood ere Thou canst
limn with it?"

I entered the house. There was the crippled daughter, her body contorted, her knees pressed to her chin as if in a vise, a terrible grip which would persist for years. I was profoundly struck by her optimism as I handed her some remembrances from the Guild.

She smiled at the gentle irony of it all. She had earned gifts for many others at the benefits in which she herself had participated. She had freely contributed her talents and kindnesses to less fortunate ones.

"I am happy, Father. I know I look terrible, but I receive Communion frequently; that's everything to me. And I have my books, and Dad over there is my constant slave. I'm really glad this all happened."

Her heroism led us into the "why" of suffering. Here was the erstwhile favorite of her crowd, crippled in limb, stripped of the beauty which was her livelihood, still able to acknowledge that her soul might have twisted away from the grasp of God had this thing not happened to her. It was a bitter, but a merciful, cross.

Soon after, the Actors Guild held another Benefit. It proved to be Helen Morgan's last. This time the crippled girl could not be included on the bill. The Drake Hotel in Chicago was jammed. Everyone looked forward to Helen's arrival. Many began to wonder if she'd make it. The Guild President was obviously disturbed with all the questions.

"She'll get here — don't worry. Anyway, look at who's here — Mitzi Green, Simone Simone, Joey Fay, Mary Brian, Hal Leroy, Fran Allison, Marty May. You want more than that?"

Our fears were not groundless. Helen arrived very late. Most of the guests had departed, grumbling as they went.

She stood in the lobby of the Hotel, the picture of

apology, with a long ermine coat wrapped regally about her thin, trembling form. It was no use pressing the point that she had failed us. She had so often helped before.

"Father, I just couldn't make it." We knew that her regrets were as real as herself, and that she was sick.

Two months later a hurried call came in to the Holy Name Cathedral from Henrotin hospital. The great singer was dying. She had never been baptized. She wanted a priest to hurry over and give her the sacraments. Eight days later she died; no doubt she was greatly welcomed in the place which is celebrated for its heavenly music. Father Regan, who attended her, mentioned a serious distraction about music. As he said the final prayers, the strains of "Just My Bill" kept intruding on his solemn liturgical Latin.

On the pages of the big sick-call book resting on the counter in the Cathedral office, are thousands of names, each one carrying a story. One especially catches the eye, because it is so short.

"Helen Morgan: Baptized; Holy Communion; Extreme Unction; Last Blessing."

The drama is locked within the bracket of a week. Its key, however, dangles back into the past, to another book, where it is written:

"Blessed are the merciful; for they shall obtain mercy."

# High Hat and Calamity

A LOW moan snaps me back to the present. The cat!
The old rascal, still on trial, rears up like a diminutive
pony, and twirls his bandage about in a queer, pawing
sort of dance. He catches cold disapproval in my glance
and settles back to nurse his wounds. The usually warm-
hearted housekeeper appears for a moment. She looks at
the cat, and his eyes flutter up in quick hope, like a
criminal's would on the night of his execution when any
interruption might mean a reprieve from the governor.

But it is Good Friday and a terrible thing has happened. The air is freighted with the undertones of scan-

dal. The cat stands up as if to steady himself for what
he thinks is a new onslaught. His one good ear takes in
enough, however, to make him relax. He listens with a
sly nod of satisfaction as the housekeeper bubbles out
details. He was disturbingly like his human masters
in hearing about someone else being in the soup for a
change.

"Father, it was awful! The church so beautiful and
everything — everybody was there . . ." And she went
on to picture the situation as only one in her strategic
position could. The members of the Mother Connelly
Guild and Holy Name Society and Altar and Rosary
Sodality were all present for their hours of adoration,
through Holy Thursday night into the next morning.

"We were all there. Just as the sun came up, that
woman down the street gave me her deep-freeze look
again. I was awfully ashamed when it happened. I told
you, Father, all the time, no good will ever come — "

I cut her short with good reason. I couldn't afford to
have her sputter on to the climax, which I now felt deep
in my bones. What she was talking about was the new
cat (we had two now). Some children had appeared at
the door a year or so before with the fluffy little waif
and begged me to adopt it.

"It is a pedigree, Father, honest it is. You should see
the mother! She is beautiful and so gentle and well be-
haved and good. We named it 'Blackie.' "

Ignoring the inference that I needed some neutralizing
animal influence in the rectory, I took the coal black kitten
into the family. From the beginning, the people were
happy about it.

"Now at least," said a troublesome wag, "we won't have the wild cat in our church all the time. The pastor would be smart if he kept the old devil out of sight."

Ogden Nash, the poet, lamented once that
> "The trouble with a kitten is that
> It eventually becomes a cat."

With Blackie it was different. As he grew into adulthood he grew apace in the estimation of the parishioners. He had a soft, silky pelt, which resembled a fine sealskin from Saks Fifth Avenue. He walked into church with the greatest of reverence. His gait was majestic — no hurry, no vulgar galloping around the sanctuary — just right for a pastor's cat. He was a blueblood and he knew it.

He went visiting throughout the parish. I suspected mild sarcasm in being told so often by housewives that they loved to have this new cat visit them for the day.

"The children love him. He's a real gentleman," they'd tell me.

He would regularly attend meetings of the sodalities. Some of the officers had frequently entertained him. He liked to be present at their more serious discussions. He acted as if he knew more about the question before the house than the ladies themselves. It got so that someone suggested that he should pick up stubs for the door prizes.

"We might get a real honest shake for a change."

The Sisters over at the convent were more discreet in expressing their delight over the newcomer's undoubted gifts. Mother Eugene, the Superior, remained loyal to the discredited tomcat, who seemed to be biding his time, hoping that Blackie would stumble over his pride. For years she had taught some rough little characters in an eastern city and her sympathetic nature could absorb an overload of mischievous behavior, even from cats.

But the Sister Sacristan was pleased. The contrast in the conduct of the two cats was too much for her. She decorated the black beautiful one with a purple ribbon and would stealthily commend him with coy innuendos.

"You're a good one. The pastor had some sense this time, when he let you in — you're a darling all right."

St. Anthony took a stoical attitude, as statues do. He didn't get much attention any more, except an occasional swipe over his sandals by the cleaning woman. He appeared to miss the personalized treatment from his four-legged feather duster, who had long since been discouraged by slaps and reprimands from the precincts of the church.

The organist, who habitually exuded emotion, was much pleased. Blackie would arrive in the choir loft with the dignity of a first nighter at the opera. If the singing was raucous, he would leave in undisguised disgust. If the melodies were pleasing to him, he would stay until the end, purring his approval.

Having a celebrity in the house had its drawbacks. The Irish maid, whose family back home had three dogs and four cats in the house, couldn't understand why Blackie wouldn't eat ordinary three-for-a-quarter cans of horse-meat. Special fish delicacies had to be prepared for him. We tried to justify this deference to his fancy by thinking of him as an ambassador of good will in charge of public relations. And he was also sartorially correct: silk coat, top hat, tail, and all.

The janitor, also from the old country, took a jaundiced view of Blackie's extraterritorial privileges. "Cat's ain't supposed to do nothing but catch rats and mice," he complained. "Not just walk around, putting on airs, like one of them aristocrats."

The opinion of the priests in the rectory was discreetly divided. The older assistant, a very patient man, without pinpointing anything in particular, read aloud at the table one evening from an article in *The Pastoral Review,* which decried the presence of too many animal pets in the parish house. It pointed out that there was grave danger at times that a dog, for instance, might receive preferential treatment over the curates.

But Blackie by now had reached an eminence well beyond the searchlights of criticism. His salesmanship was at an all time high. His hauteur was even praised as only right in one who had reached such a lofty pedestal.

Of course he had not deigned to look at the Holy Week schedule hanging on the wall of the sacristy, which gave directions on devotions to the ordinary people of the parish. I squirmed as I listened to my housekeeper finish giving the facts.

The old gray and tan cat had moved closer to my desk, and stared at me. He had flung away his bandage to allow more freedom for the chilling argument for the defense. It was calculated to snow me under; and it did.

"You and that young, black, high-hat hypocrite!" he seemed to say. "He's as hollow as that shiny pipe you're smoking. I might be a rogue; but I'm not a renegade. I never ate meat on Friday — not a mouse, anyway, in front of the whole congregation in the middle of the sanctuary and on Good Friday — of all days!"

He smirked up at me with that insufferable "I told you so" look in his green eyes.

# Stealing Home

PHENOMENA of grace seemed commonplace in the
Chicago ward called the 42nd. Crime commissions became concerned when they found that it had more vice
per square block than any ward in any city in the
Middle West.

Its many saloons were frowzy symbols of its decadence.
The floor shows, geared to the taste of gullible conventioneers, were offensive parades of paganism. Knockout
drops, dope peddling, sluggings and "heistings" were part
and parcel of the night. It would be difficult to see how
any good could come from all of this.

A little to the south, however, respectable places did
a legitimate business. Like oases on a desert of disrepute,
they catered to the normal thirsty man with giant steins
and free food for all. One particular tavern drew the

sports crowd and also an evangelist, who frequented the saloon, not for beer, but with the gospels on his tongue. He had a reputation for planting the yeast of suggestion into the hearts of his worldly hearers.

One day, I would find myself in the final culturing of that leaven which had possibly been planted in the man behind the bar long before I could even spell out "conspiracy of grace." His name was Fred Pfeffer, and he presided over his place in a genial, satisfied way. Fred Pfeffer had a record, which ranked with the best of baseball's immortals. His arm, which now slid foaming beakers across the mahogany bar, had been classed as one of the best. The Cubs' record book tells the impressive story:

"Nathanial Frederick Pfeffer, born March 17, 1860; sixteen years in Major League ball: the Cubs (White Stockings), 1883–1891, Giants, 1896, Cubs, 1897. Second baseman, by trade; also shortstop, outfielder, pitcher. Hit .325 in 1887. Died, April 10, 1932."

Happily, the evangelist, Billy Sunday, was a fly chaser on the same team from 1883 to 1887. Naturally Pfeffer became a target for Billy's barrage of spiritual counsel. Pfeffer's later married life was uneventful. His serious little wife became a convert and prayed constantly for her famous husband, continuing perhaps the frequent proddings of his old preacher friend. One spring day, she stopped at the rectory.

"Fred's dying — he has decided to enter the Church."

Fred lay quietly on his narrow cot. His face, gaunt and weatherbeaten, was relaxed in reverence. As I anointed his gnarled right hand, I thought that this decision was the most perfect strike he ever threw.

If ever a wake can be delightfully interesting, Fred Pfeffer's was. A generation of baseball's greats crowded about the coffin and exchanged old memories. They told of Fred's throwing a ball across the field or over the plate with blinding speed. He played any position with equal grace. His bat was feared by every pitcher in the league.

They reminisced about the persistent Billy Sunday, who had promised to preside at Fred's funeral. He would be present, for sure, but in the pew as a pall bearer. As usual with baseball people, someone had to top the story.

"Looks like Fredie's still a good switch hitter; he will be buried after a requiem high Mass tomorrow."

For once I didn't need to dig up sermon material. Pfeffer's friends had supplied the text and the content.

There were old-time fans taking in the details of the church services. They admired Pfeffer and were human enough to want to be present at even a sad gathering of baseball's "Who's Who." Among the mourners were pitchers, catchers, fielders, umpires, grounds keepers. In the front pew sat Billy Sunday. He looked satisfied but somewhat surprised about Fred's final tally.

Obviously the sermon should be geared to the scene of Fred's last stolen base.

"Life is a game. The paths around the bases are well defined. No one is sure about the score in the end; but the odds are heavily on the side of the players. God supplies the 'go,' plainly marks out directions, grants the power to complete the trip. Some get a walk. The next batter might homer into the stands for a pleasant jog around the diamond. More often, there is trouble along the line. Some never quite make first base, others are spiked storming into second. Others get the breaks and make it easily to home.

"Occasionally, a man comes through with the most spectacular play of all. Jumping back and forth at third, it is anybody's guess if he'll make it or not. The enemy, crafty and adroit, tries to catch him off stride. The catcher fires back to slow him down.

"Then, like a flash, the slide — the cloud of dust — the outstretched arms of the eternal Judge.

"Safe!"

# More Thefts

THE 42nd Ward also intrigued one Dempster Mac-Murphy, who liked to play cops and robbers. His keen newspaper nose put him on the scent of many a good story. He walked the streets in tireless search for something new. He rode with the police on their nightly prowls. He seemed to seek a height he never could quite attain.

Until one day, he found it on a far distant hill. It was long ago. On it were two thieves. He felt as if he personally watched from afar.

He saw them hanging beside the Nazarene, looking fearfully at the crowd milling about their feet. They curse the soldiers who permit men and women to jostle up against them to heighten their pain and increase the humiliation of their fate.

Suddenly above the din there is a chorus of shouts which rises in an ever increasing crescendo above the noise: "If Thou art the Son of God, come down from the Cross. If Thou art the Son of God, save Thyself and us."

One of the thieves joins savagely in the outcry. The other is strangely moved. He sees the sweet outlines of the face so close to his, how He almost smiles in His agony as if He pities the crowd and feels the temptation to step down and again walk in their midst.

In quick rebuke, he flares in anger at the other thief, "This man has done no wrong."

Then by some queer stealth of grace, he recognizes his God. He pulls at his ropes and leans close to Christ.

"Lord, remember me when Thou shalt come into Thy kingdom."

It is perhaps his first prayer — and his last.

What paradox! In all the delirium of that hysterical day, a thief lifted his voice in recognition — and Christ who would not speak to the high priest who represented His Father on earth, Christ who remained silent before the prying eyes of Herod, who never answered the taunt: "Come down from the cross," spoke to this wretched man who dared all in one desperate act of fair play. Christ smiled at him and gave him the key to His heavenly abode.

"This day thou shalt be with Me in Paradise."

This criminal, personally sainted by Christ, had been taking short cuts all his life. The easy dollar, the soft drachma was the keynote of his life until he recognized the most important haul of his career. He escaped from the imprisonment of earth and slipped past the gates of Paradise with the key of true repentance. One of the precious seven last words of Christ was reserved for a crook who saved himself with astonishing dexterity under the impact of Divine Grace.

It is strange that devotion to the penitent thief did not catch fire until the twentieth century. Certainly this was not determined by any lack of thieves who purloin their way through society in prodigious numbers.

Penitentiaries are filled with the small percentage who have been caught up to by the long arm of the law. Over this group, hovers a certain pall of despair. Short timers think of their release. Some plan foolproof escapes; others just languish in the depths of gloom.

Perhaps Christ thought of these harassed souls as He looked on Dismas ending his life on the hill of sacrifice. His natural impulse was one of gratitude and of course it was normal for Him to be royal in His beneficence, drawing a thief from the tortures of death to the bliss of the beatified, from the bitterness of the cross to the sweet fruit of Paradise. He was personally the Redeemer of all men. He wanted to save this wastrel who epito- mized the millions of other wretches who would take up the cudgels of crime.

Because Christ could see into the future, He might have been comforted a bit by the sudden vision of a twentieth-century movement which would recognize the significance of Dismas. It would make Dismas a definite source of hope in a day which would be filled with murder, rapine, hate, genocide, contentions, and just plain sin.

Dempster MacMurphy, a southerner with no particular hankering for theology, "the cops and robber man," did more than anyone to build this citadel around him. We who knew Dempster MacMurphy remembered him as unpredictable and radiantly lighthearted.

In Dallas, Texas, where he was born and named Dempster Ostrander Murphy, there is a single grave, which, with a membership in a clothes-pressing club, was his only possession when he died in 1932. That was the year he began to make a posthumous comeback as spectacular as that of his beloved hoodlum saint.

Some years before, he had come to Chicago, and soon became vice-president of the Insull Utilities. At this time he decided to change his name — just why no one knew. Perhaps he felt that there were too many meat and potato Murphys in Chicago. But there was no MacMurphy listed in the telephone directory.

The presence of millions of dollars worth of securities signed with "MacMurphy" got Samuel Insull into high dudgeon. He had to haul MacMurphy over to Superior Court to legalize him. Millions in securities were invalidly issued under the new name of the puckish vice-president.

However his alias will be remembered long after Insull's stocks have molded in the graveyard of worthless early '30's investments, because MacMurphy remembered Dismas.

With the Insull Empire in ruins, MacMurphy was out

of a job. He slept in trains in the winter time and on park benches with the derelicts in the summer months. As he watched the stars at night, he often thought of the good thief and the mercy of Christ toward this down and out man.

"He was a sinner," Dempster would say. "I haven't much patience with other kinds of people. Not only that, he was the only saint ever canonized by Christ or by papal curia or by Christendom, who isn't positive of his own name."

It was not too hard for him to like the bum on Golgotha when looking at the heavens from the observatory of a park bench, surrounded by the drifters of a world which had forgotten how to live.

MacMurphy can never be accused of not trying to do something about the dismal qualities of this little world. One time when still a student in the East, he happened across an oratorical contest in full swing. He got into the act and carried off first prize, although he was in- eligible. At Georgetown University in Washington, the pixie in him took hold. He played hooky and became a song and dance man in a theatrical unit. When he de- cided to join the Catholic Church in the capital city, he studied with an intense zeal; and he carried a keen spiritual enthusiasm to the grave.

Obviously a man of MacMurphy's kidney could not remain supine on a bench. With the thief leading the way, he found his true métier.

Three years after his tumble from financial heights, he became business manager of the Chicago *Daily News*.

On his trips to the office he was an easy target for pan-handlers who could recognize a "softy" ten leagues away. He never turned a beggar down.

"Maybe he was a vice-president once," he would say in answer to the jibes of the smarter folk.

MacMurphy began his campaign for Dismas from scratch. No one felt particularly sorry for the thief. After all, he pulled up with a record second to none.

"A queer bird this Dismas," Edwin Lahey, a Chicago *Daily News* feature writer and friend of MacMurphy, wrote. "Dempster MacMurphy brought him to light several years ago in the columns of the *Daily News,* taking him out of obscurity that had enveloped him for more than nineteen hundred years, since that spring day on Calvary when the thief on the cross forgot his own suffering long enough to throw a friendly word to a stranger suffering the same death, a stranger whom Dismas felt was taking a bum rap."

Lahey continued: "Dismas is the only saint I know of who doesn't offer you two for one. Every other saint seems to have a jurisdiction in which there is a payoff. St. Christopher protects the traveler, St. Anthony finds lost money, and so on down the line. Too often the saints are touted up to be specialty merchants for supplying the specific needs of hungry and selfish human beings."

Despite Lahey's remarks, Dismas began to have a clientele on that day when he recognized his God. Thousands of prisoners have rallied around the drama of the cross and clung desperately to its lesson. Lifers could see life beyond. Thieves could visualize salvation in repentance.

Outcasts could catch the sight of home in the heavenly mansion, which had room for the thief who had made straight his ways.

When Dempster MacMurphy died, his name became legendary as belonging to a man who had emphasized the workings of grace among criminals. A chapel was dedicated to Dismas at Dannemora, New York. A fund is operating in memory of MacMurphy to aid the needy and to promote devotion among prisoners. Pope Pius XII, in 1953, granted permission to celebrate a Good Thief Sunday Mass each year in American penal institutes. (To have a Mass entered into the liturgical year is a most extraordinary thing.) The Gospel of that Sunday tells the story which inflamed the heart of this man of our own day, who was himself condemned for a time to an outcast company.

Edwin A. Lahey's epitaph to the soul of this amazing combination of ardor and faith follows:

"At the age of 42, MacMurphy died in Battle Creek, Michigan, hopeful of teaming up with his beloved Dismas and scoring some assists on those 'shoestring catches in the outfield of eternity.'"

# The Badge and the Beads

DEMPSTER MacMURPHY'S death brought a sorrow to the many persons who considered him a curious bit of color in the murky canvas of the 42nd Ward. The police officers of the Chicago Avenue station particularly missed him.

On week ends the jail was usually crowded with arrests. A bedraggled group of men and women would stand before the sergeant with the same old complaints and would get the same old advice. MacMurphy, who was often present at these cursory trials, would jump up with the vehemence of a sawdust trail evangelist, and deliver a sermon on vagrancy and sin. The case-hardened old loafers would shuffle to attention. It was the closest most of them ever came to a pulpit.

One of the officers was Sergeant O'Dowd. He was a big man, inside and out.

"He was as good as old Canon McShea in his prime," he would tell his fellow officers, thinking of those days, when he himself, was spiritually moved by MacMurphy's eloquence. "And our old parish priest in County Mayo was one who could charm the birds out of the trees, too, if he put a mind to it."

On his last day on the police force the sergeant was having a usually troublesome afternoon. He thought he would say his beads for a while. That drunken, blasphemous wretch in cell 3, was swearing like all get-out.

"A Hail Mary, or two will please God, and maybe take the curse off the place," he mumbled to himself.

"Hail, Mary, full of Grace . . ." His large red fingers closed around his rosary.

A violent scream of hate drilled through the corridor.

"Lemme outta this old rattrap, you big copper!"

"You'll be in again and again, woman, if you don't behave yourself. All you got to do is keep your hands out of other people's pocketbooks," O'Dowd shouted back.

"Hail, Mary, full of Grace, the Lord is with thee . . ."

It was good to think of the angel Gabriel, all bright and shiny, in the quiet little room at Nazareth; and "The

Lady" looking up with her lovely eyes, quiet like, and she just a wee girl, knowing that the good Lord would soon come to her blessed bosom.

"Say, O'Dowd — how about cutting a hand or two? It's getting awful dull in here," a voice broke in.

"Get along with you, Smith. You're as crooked as a dog's hind leg. I wouldn't cut a string with the likes of you."

The card sharp sat on the bench across the room dealing from a stacked deck to an invisible partner. He was keeping fit while he waited for his bail. His lush, gambling den on Wells Street had been raided again. He shook his head. It was getting unreasonable, these complaints from suspicious customers.

"As always, O'Dowd, you're a consummate bigot," he said.

". . . Blessed art thou among women and blessed is the fruit of thy womb, Jesus," the sergeant went on.

" 'Twas a pity that the little maid couldn't find a place to put the Infant Jesus. Too bad He didn't decide to be born in his little Irish village. There'd a' been a roof over His head and a spot of tea for His Blessed Mother."

The sergeant sighed as he seemed to hear the swish of the spray across the rocks. He could see the craggy, bending coast line and the mountains of Connamara, rising like misty cathedral spires from the floor of the sea; and the thatched houses all along the way, with the smoke from the peat, curling blue and cozy like, through the squat chimneys; the hill of CroaghPatrick, rising above the town, where the great saint threw the bell down the green slopes after the snakes. He was "missing these hills, now, missing them awful." The sergeant came up with a start.

Someone in the far section was pounding on the iron bars with a pipe. O'Dowd felt for a second that he was tumbling down CroaghPatrick with a hundred bells clanging at his heels. But the noise was made by the thug who had beaten his victim unmercifully.

"He was a bad one all right," thought the sergeant as he recalled the report on the brutal robbery.

"Hush, you!" O'Dowd was red with fury at having his dreams so shattered. "I'll lather you good if you don't shut up." He settled back again.

"'. . . Holy Mary, Mother of God, pray for us sinners . . .'

"Only for the Grace of God," he thought, "I would be back in those cells, instead of sitting comfortably enough in this position of authority. There were plenty of sinners around, dear God, to keep You pretty busy in this district. It must be hard for You tagging after the likes of them, with their guns, with their hard hearts, and them shouting and clawing away like a pack of Kilkenny cats. It must have been tough to see Your Mother crying and sobbing when You carried that heavy cross and them hollering after You like bloody savages. You were awful goodhearted to turn to Your Father to forgive them, because they knew not what they did. Too bad though a few of us stout men from Mayo weren't around to help You out."

The prisoners decided to combine their nuisance values and let go all at once. They shouted, cursed, hammered away at the walls. Their insults nearly succeeded in bringing O'Dowd to his feet. The hackles of his anger rose and fell like the bellows in his father's blacksmith shop; but he was moved with a great pity. He was getting soft he guessed.

". . . Holy Mary, Mother of God, pray for us sinners now and at the hour of our death . . ." he said. The hour of death had been very real to him so often. He was sixty-three now. He looked at his desk. The boys had brought him presents of candy and cigarettes for his birthday.

"You can retire now, Terrence. You're deserving of a rest. Thirty-eight years in uniform is plenty. You can make that trip back home," they said.

He was pleased with their good will and with many other things, especially for having had his good wife so long. God rest her. He was pleased with all the children. It had been hard to raise them all. There was nothing left of his salary to go on holidays; but maybe now he could, with most of them married, and with the youngest, Kathleen, God be praised, a nun, safe and sound in a convent in Milwaukee.

The clamor ceased. The card sharp muttered something like "your deal." The drunken man groaned a little and fell back. The sergeant's eyes grew misty. Far away he could see the outlines of his father's house and the shop next door, the horses, the donkeys waiting to be shod. His father Fergus O'Dowd had been a huge man too, with a shock of red hair, which would brush across his blue eyes as he stooped over to hammer on the iron shoes. He was blessed with a pair of hands which could bend a thick steel bar in mid-air. He could throw the weights at the County Fair farther than anyone in the West. No one ever picked a quarrel with Fergus. He was quiet and patient. But only a fool would chance bringing the mild man's anger to a head.

"Terrence," he said one day. "Your passage to America is all set. I'll be missing ye more than I'll be admittin'. Your brothers are in Chicago ahead of ye. They'll find work for ye, maybe on the police force."

The great hand of the smithy brushed back his hair, and with it a laggard tear.

"You're twenty-three now. They'll be no opportunity left here for ye. Remember you've the divil's own temper. Keep it down — ye'll be in a strange country and on your own. God go with ye, Son, and may His Blessed Mother keep ye good and clean."

The sergeant shifted uneasily as he remembered his first years on the police department, adjusting himself to the ways of the new world; and then his transfer to the Chicago Avenue district, one of the toughest in the city. His talents recommended him to dangerous assignments among the criminal elements on the Near North Side. He was an expert pistol shot. He had earned civic and newspaper awards for heroism under fire. His name became almost legendary in the street warfare of the neighborhood.

His prolonged distraction with the past brought him a twinge of conscience. He focused again on the solemn words of the Our Father and the Hail Mary; but before putting full mind to them, he interposed a prayer of gratitude.

"But thanks be to God, I never killed a man and as I see it from here, I did a fine job reaching the age of sixty-three without getting killed meself."

"Our Father, Who art in heaven, hallowed be Thy Name . . ."

A dinner plate wheeled across the floor and cracked up against the card sharp's feet. He jumped up and stomped about on the scattered deck and bits of crockery.

"This is the worst run jail I've ever seen," he ranted. "If I were running it I'd have you all hanged by the heels."

O'Dowd bristled. "Quiet, boy, you're not running it."

A lockup man made the rounds of the cells and restored some order, but the drunken man continued to cry out in agony.

"I can't stand it — please let me out — I'm dying."

The sergeant rose from his chair. His fine frame moved toward cell No. 3.

"Leonard, take over for a minute," he said to a young man who had just entered the room. Leonard was a new officer, about to become a part of that scene which O'Dowd was soon to leave.

He unlocked the door and sat beside the man who lay on a bench twisting about in agony. His eyes, bloodshot and rolling with fear, looked at the sergeant's large figure next to him.

"I'll hold you for a while. You'll be all right, my boy. Try to relax a little," O'Dowd said.

The man leaned back and seemed to feel the solid hand of hope.

"God help me," he moaned. "God help me."

O'Dowd leaned over and whispered with the soothing confidence of one who knew.

"He will, . . . son. He will — He always does."

After a few minutes O'Dowd got up and walked out. He paused at the door of the station and looked around. Some officers came up from the rear. A squad car had emptied out. Three men and a woman were brought in between two policemen. They tried to wrench themselves free.

He had so often seen the struggles between the forces of law and the forces of evil, the policemen reluctantly using the clubs of their profession and their captives fighting them off like tigers at bay. O'Dowd was saddened by the familiar scene of his men doggedly pursuing their duty and the men and the woman who had failed in their duty to society and their God.

O'Dowd breathed a prayer: "God help them." He was feeling lonely in the midst of the scuffling, the loud voices and the pity of it all. He waited for a pause and said, "So long, boys, I'm going home now."

He stepped out into the street and looked back.

His last day. A shock of red hair fell across his blue eyes. His great hand brushed it back, and with it a laggard tear.

"I'll be missing you, missing you all a lot," he whispered to himself. He walked, steady and strong, toward the west.

# The Barber and Dreams

THE old gray building on the south side of Chicago Avenue is not only a police station. It is an archive, containing weird and assorted material on crime. The hoodlum empire which kept the station's force on the jump for a decade, gradually eliminated itself in an unprecedented civil war of extermination. Rival mobsters rhythmically machine gunned themselves into the grave, where any clues to their crimes were generally clamped down forever beneath the lids of $10,000 coffins.

The written reports on these murders, like all vital statistics, were as cold as the tombstones over the bodies of the many victims concerned. They did not interest themselves with the many human dramas which threaded through that crazy quilt of a mixed-up era.

Not all of these ended in the grave, however, at least not in the grave of vanished hopes. I remember the death of the gangster's widow and the different route she took from the one leading through tangled maze of the underworld. The widow's husband was a racketeer by trade, and like many of his kind, met death in gangland fashion. The newspapers had a field day in describing the grisly aspects of his "last ride." The motive seemed to be money, some $150,000 in cash, which the police were also interested in locating.

His widow, who managed to survive her grief, rented an apartment over a barber shop on Chicago Avenue. Her journey from a sordid past, ended in this spot. But before she died, she had a dream which no one would believe, especially the barber, who also had a dream, which his friends in turn did not believe until both dreams came true. The barber still cannot believe that he had much to do with the widow's dream coming true. His instruments were a razor, a scissors, and a gift for conversation, which became quite unbelievably an instrument of grace.

Over the door of the barber shop, a sign in bold letters announced that here you could "get the best haircut in town." The two chairs were always busy. The customers were not so intrigued by the promise of tonsorial excellence as they were by the camaraderie of the place. Joe

and Tony were co-owners and absolute lords of their domain. Joe was very quiet and always looked absorbed in
his work. He dressed in a neat white jacket and seemed
much like a learned scientist, about to explore the skull of
a prehistoric man. Probably he had long since given up
the hope of expressing himself much.

Tony took care of public opinion. It didn't bother him
that his broken English sometimes derailed his train of
thought. His ideas were as sound as the flashing shears
which he would whirl about when he needed to stab
home a point.

Many priests from the Cathedral patronized the shop.
One learned professor who had studied in Rome, used to
try out his Italian on Tony, who would shake his head
in amazement.

"Gee, Fadder, you talk better Italian than me."

Any mention of Italy would start Tony on an emotional
tour of his mother country.

"I gotta take a trip back some day — I gotta meet people over there — they write me all the time. They say
'Come over, Tony, quick, we'll show you the best time of
your life.'"

No one took him seriously, except a woman who peered
in through the window one day, beneath the words "Best
Haircut In Town." I happened to be seated in one of the
chairs waiting my turn. The woman's face pressed against
the pane. Her dark, olive skin blanched as she took in the
presence of the priest. Tony, with the facile patter of a
gossip columnist, explained,

"She's the wife of the guy who got the works last
month."

He stepped to the door and waved.

"Come on in and meet the Fadder. You better be good — he'll get after you if you don't watch out."

Despite the discouraging note in the barber's introduction, she entered and sat down for a while. She didn't seem to mind Tony's rather noisy solicitude for her soul. Joe, with his usual diplomacy, moved around his chair with embarrassment. He would have approached the question of her reform with more finesse.

"You'll never get to heaven if you don't look out."

The woman tried to say something in between the volley of advice.

After a few moments she rose and managed to say: "Guess I'll be goin'. Pleased to meet you, Father. . . . Funny, Tony, last night I dreamt I went to heaven."

Everyone was silent as she left; but not for long.

"She looks in here every day. I always tell her the priest asks for her — a little lie you know, Fadder — but she's awfully happy when I say that. She was pretty bad once, I guess. She thinks she ain't good enough to go to church. I tell her that's a lot of crazy stuff to say things like that — ain't I right, Fadder?"

Time passed. Several miles of hair fell to the floor of the barber shop; and if it had been possible to record it on tape there would have been many more miles of conversation.

It would have been recorded that every day the anxious woman had looked in through the window to see if a priest was there. She would enter to meet the same questions: "How about it, Lois? How about it? The Fadder's been asking for you."

One day the answer was disarming. The barber was not prepared to handle it as expertly as he was the normal developments of his day.

"Tony, I went back to church. I know you'd like to hear that. I try to go every day now. Thanks, Tony, thanks a lot."

"Well, I'll be darned." Tony smiled. "I can't believe it. Well, I'll be darned!"

Tony would soon fly over the ocean. For weeks before his trip, his imagination flared into far-off places as he stropped his razor.

"I'll eat like a king. I'll see the Pope. I'll look up all my friends . . ."

His customers were willing to go along with his extravagant dreams. "Tony believes in gremlins and fairy queens," said one of them.

A huge airliner droned over the sea, homeward bound from Rome. It carried the Cardinal Archbishop of Chicago who was returning from a Holy Year visit to the Eternal City. Some years before he had received the Red Hat from the hands of Pope Pius XII. It was symbolic of his exalted station. He was a prince of the Church, a spiritual empire which extended back into the very twilight of history, long before the royal houses of Europe and the dynasties of the East had risen. The Cardinal sat contentedly watching the clouds scud by. His secretary, a young clergyman, and several members of the party, talked glowingly about their trip. Toward the back of the plane, a man and a woman were conversing in fluent Italian. The secretary seemed to recognize the voice.

"It couldn't be," he thought. "Not Tony!"

He got to his feet to make sure.

The barber's eyes lighted up in recognition and delight; "Monsignor — this is somethin'! Oh, pardon me — I would like to introduce to you a good friend."

He bowed to an elegantly dressed lady, who evidently was a woman of culture.

"Monsignor, the Principessa Maria. She would like to meet the Cardinal."

The clergyman fumbled for words. The princess of one of the most noble and ancient houses in Rome with the proprietor of the shop where you could get the best haircut in town! It was a little staggering.

"He would be delighted to meet you, Princess."

The formal introduction was made. The Prince of the church and the Principessa talked for a while. Tony stood back, uncommonly silent, enjoying the triumph of his life. Then he stepped forward and began a spirited conversation with the Cardinal and his staff, thinking all the time how he would tell the story of his exalted acquaintanceships to his customers.

Back in his shop again, he talked with unusual gusto and now his opinions had gained immense authority. He was a man whose dreams had come true. No one in his right mind would dare question the veracity of the man. He had plenty of clergymen to back up his latest story.

"He could have been hanging around with prime ministers and kings for all I know," the one-time skeptic said.

One day we received a call. It was about the woman who had lived above the barber shop. She had died suddenly, and just before, had asked for the priest, as she had looked for him so many times before. The police had searched her threadbare apartment, still looking for the $150,000. She had died without a penny. Over on her desk lay a half finished letter; it said that her greatest desire since her return to the Sacraments was to be buried at Mass. She knew that we would understand.

There were five or six people in the Holy Name Cathedral on the morning of the funeral. The Catholic Charities had given us money to buy her coffin. It looked little and lonely there, in the wide aisle, which led to the sanctuary of God. Back of it sat the little barber, with his eyes glued ahead, no laughter now or talking about his dreams.

He was thinking of the time she had said: "Funny, Tony, last night I dreamt I went to heaven."

## Around the Edges

IN 1871, the Chicago fire swept away the frame structure which had served as the Cathedral. In 1876, the new Holy Name Cathedral was nearing completion. Since then its spire, tall and slim, has pointed steadily up to God in silent witness of the personal and public history of so many people and events.

The ceremonies within its hallowed walls have always been fittingly beautiful. Chicago has had its share of great religious celebrations. They form a saga of unbelievable religious growth, from 400 catholics in 1843 with their bishop and a handful of priests, to the diocese of today, which ranks as the largest in the Western Hemisphere. These events of course are well recorded.

What will never be fully written down are the curious episodes which swing around the edges of the ceremonies, about the men and women who function behind the scenes.

Sacristans are always essential cogs in the mechanism of the church. Where so many religious events took place, there were always minute preparations and then the drudgery of cleaning up and rearranging after the scene had been enacted. Then only the smell of incense lingered in the air, as the vigil lights penciled red through the lazy shafts of smoke which still clung around the majestic altar; and the sacristan padded about the sanctuary, seeing that everything was in order for tomorrow.

One of these sacristans was a short, thin man from Armenia. His name was Michael. He was a faithful watchman besides being a zealous worker. He lived close by and would make his way through the bustling crowds in the street and happily enter the church for his daily tasks. When the old rector, Msgr. Fitzsimmons died after a long career, and lay in state in the middle aisle of the cathedral for several days and nights, dressed in his priestly vestments, priests and laymen from all over the country came to look for the last time upon his distinguished face.

Michael, "the Dark Angel," as the sacristan was called because of his complexion and unquestioned piety, would not leave the church. When the other mourners left and the lights were dimmed, he remained on guard. Overcome with fatigue, he fell asleep several times on the carpet next to the cardinal's throne. But he was at home

with the prelate whom he loved as he was at home before
the tabernacle with the vigil lights flickering away. They
seemed to suggest: "You are in your Father's house and
it is good to be here even in the dark — which is only the
prelude to the dawn."

Michael the "Dark Angel," was succeeded by another
devoted sacristan, who was born in Newfoundland, where
during his boyhood he had often hunted wild game; and
like the youngsters of the country lived without alarm in
the vicissitudes of a wilderness. When he came to Chicago
and rented an apartment across from Cathedral Square
to be close to his work, he developed a wholesome fear
of the neighborhood. After all, he argued, the bullets are
leveled at men and not at game in this territory. His ap-
prehensions proved logical.

When he was in his apartment, he could hear people in
the rooms above, their muffled voices, the shuffling of
feet, men coming and going. One night police cars
screeched around the building. Spotlights flared across
the front and back and blinded him as he peered out into
the streets. He couldn't believe it. One of the biggest
narcotic rings of the decade had been operating above
him all the time. He watched the dark figures being
pushed into the cars. They were gone, but not his yearn-
ings for the wilderness of his boyhood home. For years
afterward, he was never sure of himself except when he
walked about the calm inside of the Cathedral on his endless chores.

The organ loft at the rear of the Cathedral had an orbit
all its own. In it swung another world, quite distinct from

the splendid, perfect liturgical services up front. The
weeks of preparation for jubilees, the dozens of men and
boy singers who tramped up the winding stairs to line up
around the organ, the symphony orchestras which backed
up the choristers, the priest directors who were in charge
of all this music and song provided interesting departures
from what was indicated in the scores.

Usually the well-rehearsed choristers went through
their performances without incident. However, one Sunday a baffling mystery developed. As the boys left to walk
down the stairs, the priest in charge noticed that their
white linen surplices over their cassocks were slit down
the back. Everyone was questioned, from the hulking
youngster with the furtive look, to the cherubic darling of
the loft, with the big, expressive eyes and the prospect of
being another Enrico Caruso before too long.

On the following Sunday, the same thing happened.
The seamstress was ready to resign. The priest could not
keep his mind on his work. Next Sunday he watched
every motion of every hand.

"No, not the child with the cherubic eyes!" he almost
shouted as he made a lunge for the hand holding the
razor blade.

Down the stairs out into the street and across the
Square the boy fled, dressed in his cassock and surplice.
It was the last time anyone ever saw the fleeing angel
with the blade. He apparently was able to avoid forever
after coming anywhere near the scene of his unholy
operations.

L'Abbe Edgar Bourget was one of the most colorful

musical directors in our time. He was born in a small town near Quebec. After his ordination to the priesthood he was assigned to the Holy Name Cathedral to preside over the musical programs for sacred ecclesiastical functions. He was a brilliant pianist and musician. When the Cathedral was empty, he loved to sit at the organ and pour out his soul through the keys and through the great pipes which rose up around the instrument he so dearly cherished. His choir caught fire from the spirit of the little virtuoso. It became the nucleus for the celebrated choirs which his successors, Fathers Mahoney, Hoover, and Meter later brought into nationwide notice.

The Abbe had two main ambitions. One was someday to discover a genius among the singers or violinists, who could put his choir on the musical map. Then the huge crowd down below would say "Look — the Abbe's choir! Better than the Sistine, isn't it?"

The other ambition was to get out of the cold Chicago climate when his superiors would permit. He would shake all over during the cruel winter months. Even at the organ, as his hands raced over the keys, he could feel the bitter drafts and he would be yearning for the day when he could follow the sun for a while and get rid of his chills. Both ambitions doubled back on him in time. Both would end on contrasting levels in a mildly ironic way.

His search for a genius never quite succeeded. Over the years he had good singers, but he was never satisfied. The people who crowded into the church paid scant attention he thought to his mine-run choristers.

One day his spirits were lifted to dizzy heights. The well-known singer and organizer of the Chicago Opera

Co., Signor Cleo Fonte Campanini had died. Arrangements were made for his funeral in the Cathedral. The Abbe was beside himself with excitement as he practiced for the service with Campanini's good friends.

In front of him were the greatest opera stars of the day. The renowned sopranos, Galli Curci and Yvonne Gall, the Metropolitan tenors, Tito Schipa and Edward Johnston, the dramatic soprano, Rosa Raisa watched the Abbe beat out the solemn measures of Pietro Yon's requiem Mass. Here in one circle he had perhaps the finest talent ever assembled for a Mass.

"Voila! Maybe the finest ever in the world — now everybody will stare!"

The morning of the funeral arrived. It was a dismal day. But his choir was there and the artists were in fine voice. The Abbe swept the church with diapason, grace notes, motets and many other things he had carefully prepared. The Mass drew to a close. All the while he hadn't had time even to turn around. So now he got up and, swaying a little with emotion, walked over to the railing, and looked down into the church. There was just a handful of people there. What a pitifully small audience, he sighed, for his program on the one day when he had at last achieved the finest choir in the world!

Not long afterward the maestro died. His had been a vivid role in the pageantry behind the scenes. His body was brought back to the village of his birth, St. Joseph Levis, close to the waters of the St. Lawrence, now locked beneath the snow covered ice. For years there had not been a week like this. The ground was frozen solid, no spade could pierce its surface. The shield of winter lay like frosted iron on the earth. The coffin was put in a mausoleum. It must rest there until the spring.

When the doors of the great Cathedral church are locked and the crowds are gone, it could be that an organ fills the dark with brilliant swells of melody, as if it strove to find its way to the frozen North to warm the resting place of the little Abbe, who always felt the cold but never let it touch his heart.

# The Missing Name

ON THE sixth floor of the Cathedral rectory there is a long recreation room, flanked by a dining room and a kitchen. You might open the door to the south and walk onto the outdoor porch, which is always a delightful place on summer evenings.

A view from here is rewarding. Your eye traces the blazing skyline across Chicago's loop. The Merchandise Mart building, the largest building of its kind in the world, is splashed with countless lights. The shafts of the Tribune Tower and the Wrigley Building lift themselves up in an ecstasy of light toward the heavens. Farther to the south, flames from huge blast furnaces lick the sky. The sound from this labyrinth of plants, factories, business houses, hotels, railroads, motorcars always lingers and hums along in tune with the world's most cosmopolitan city.

There has been a mammoth growth, from a straggling, breezy village in the fertile prairie to this giant of industry and commerce. Your mind fades back to the few buildings and huts which once broke the steady line of the horizon to the west. Southward is the rich soil watered by the stream called Chicagou. Along its banks walked the proud Miami and Iroquois. They pitched their tents on the shores of the restless lake to the east. To the north, lay unending prairies waving their slender gloves of brown and green at the capricious winds.

Not far over on the river, there are two bronze tablets telling of these days. One reads, "In honor of Louis Joliet and Pierre Jacque Marquette, the first white men to pass through Chicago, September, 1673." A companion plaque also recalls the romantic past. It is "In honor of Rene, Cavalier, Sieur LaSalle, and Henry di Tonti, who passed through this river on their way to the Mississippi, December, 1681."

All of these intrepid men would have been startled if they had even dimly caught the vision of the towering history which would rear up on both banks of the quiet stream. It has been a far cry from the day when the daring LaSalle, with his booted foot on a rock, and his sword raised in a dramatic gesture, claimed all of this territory drained by the river and its tributaries for the king of France. That the 42nd Ward was once officially French territory is hard to imagine, as are the other memorable events which crowded through its streets.

Step back again into the room and open a well-thumbed volume — the guest book. It is a prized possession, because inked into its pages are names which have made history; others, which possibly will. It is a priceless memento of the hundreds of visitors who have walked through the Cathedral door, or around the square. The autographs of cardinals, archbishops, bishops, priests, and laymen from all over the world are held between its covers.

A volume like this has definite limitations. It can only be written in. It cannot get up and join the welcoming committees. It cannot shake hands; and especially it cannot predict the future. If it could, it presumably would have opened up by itself on occasions when no one thought about opening it to receive the autographs of certain men who came our way.

Among the distinguished prelates who visited Chicago and stayed with the Cardinal Archbishop for a few days, was Cardinal Von Preysing, the Archbishop of Berlin, who survived the horrors of two Nazi concentration camps and bore the scars of whips across his back. There was Cardinal Mindszenty, the living martyr of Hungary, who favored us with a press conference in the Cardinal's residence during his stay in Chicago. We shall not soon forget his farewell words, "I am going back now to Hungary. I am sure I shall face trumped-up charges from the courts. However, I am reconciled to the inevitable. For the sake of my people I will return."

None of us could appreciate the travesty of justice which he knew awaited him in one of the most infamous trials ever perpetrated by the enemies of Christ. His name among the Cathedral visitors is one of several which one day might be entered in the catalogue of the saints.

In October, 1936, another churchman dropped out of the skies and was greeted at Municipal Airport by a delegation of clergymen. He was about to begin a whirlwind tour of the city. He was a tall, thin, bespectacled man with deep ascetic lines etched in his face. His eyes were dark and always sparkling with affection and interest. He walked to a waiting limousine with all the grace of a noble Roman, which he was. During the many receptions and visitations, he charmed everyone with his democratic approach and his infectious warmth.

He flew from coast to coast, and finally put to sea again. In Rome, the great Pius XI was fighting through the last years of his pontificate. The prelate, just returned from the United States, sustained the aging Pope — whose secretary he was — in these last desperate hours, which were freighted with the tramp of marching feet and the hammer blows of an approaching war.

The faithful secretary knelt at the bedside of Pius XI when he died in February, 1939, and it was his sad duty to give the news of his death to the world.

On March 2, a whisp of smoke gathered over the piazza San Pietro. It vanished like the wind. But it meant that another Pope had been elected. A hundred thousand people strained to catch the name.

"We have a Pope."

It was the voice of Cardinal Dominioni, piercing the

anxious air about St. Peter's. His voice was heard instantaneously throughout all Christendom.

"It is Eugenio Pacelli."

The tall, thin, ascetic man, straight and majestic, stood before the world with the shepherd staff of Peter in his hands.

His name is missing in the cathedral guest book. No one had thought to bring it to him to autograph. No one knew that the man who walked by so fast in 1936, would be Pius XII in 1939.

# Blanche Marie

HANS RUDOLPH RHEINHARDT VON HERTZBERG
was not a creation from the Vienna woods or a name
from a Strauss operetta. The tempo of his career was not
anything like the smooth and regular tempo of a waltz.
His life progressed from wealth to poverty, from violent
torrents of passion and wild despair to the final placid
waters of faith.

Von Hertzberg in his later years lived on Clark Street

near Division in Chicago. He was a familiar figure on
these Near North Side streets. I knew of the old man first
through his initials H.R.R.H. They appeared beneath his
many book reviews and poems to Mary which he contributed to the *New World,* the official newspaper of the
archdiocese of Chicago. He was a good friend of one of
my predecessors on that paper, Father Cornelius
Donovan.

I could have missed the story behind H.R.R.H. had I
not been appointed to the paper in 1935. As managing
editor from 1940 to 1950, I struggled through the hectic
war years. Although Von Hertzberg died before Hitler
and Stalin tampered with history, his battle was one of
monumental proportions, the kind that so often happens
in the microcosm of a man's soul. I decided then and
there to investigate just how the dragnet of grace waylaid
this notorious libertine.

Fortunately his closest friend, the pastor of St. Margaret
Mary church in Chicago, was available. He had most
of his papers and manuscripts. His affection for Hans
Rudolph was deep. Nothing would please him more than
to talk about the battered derelict who mysteriously
washed up on the shores of a profound love for God and
His Virgin Mother.

It was January, 1955. Far into the night, I sat with the
priest who had been his closest companion in later years.
We were joined by a journalist who supplied more details
on Von Hertzberg's younger life when they had worked
as newspapermen in New Orleans back in 1905–1906. His
career was even more fascinating than Von Hertzberg's
— but that is a story which will come later.

"I loved the old man," the priest said. "It was an odd friendship. I met him in 1918 when I was assigned as a curate to my first parish. He was a bedraggled old man then. He saw that I was curious about his appearance. With a hearty laugh he tried to compensate by showing me a picture of himself in his dapper younger days.

"He had been handsome, suave, with a carefully waxed mustache, and a trim Van Dyke beard — very elegant. He still was distinguished looking for all his shabbiness, with clean-cut, regular features, gray hair and goatee. At the time I met him, he had no real means of support, except for some free-lance writing, some editorials and book reviews — a couple of dollars a week. He didn't seem to care.

"He was always inviting me to breakfast. He would take me to a bakery shop that had a few coffee tables in back and would treat me in the style of a southern gentleman. For fifteen cents we could get coffee, eggs, and a bun. He would preside in the grand manner, as if many servants surrounded our little repast. At these ceremonious meetings and in his disorderly room, I came to know H.R.R.H. intimately, and we became fast friends. I then learned for the first time about his devotion to "Blanche Marie." But more about that later.

"His life had been full of turmoil, grief, sin, moments of brilliance, days of awful, black gloom.

"He was born in Germany in the seventies. His parents were of the old nobility and tried to give their precocious child every opportunity for education and respectability. He was sent to France for preliminary training and was allowed to come to the United States when he was still in his teens. He enrolled at Texas University and graduated *cum laude* in law. He was an omnivorous reader and a forceful orator; and as could be expected, he tried politics. His last stand in Texas was as a district attorney. Apparently his quixotic temperament could not be satisfied even in so vast a territory as Texas.

"He was in his early thirties when he moved to New Orleans, where he worked as a columnist on the *Times Democrat* and made a hit with the public. His prose had a philosophical and earthly flavor, and he had a flare for the romantic.

"He was a thorough pagan and an atheist in his convictions. He readily admitted to me the kind of life he'd led.

" 'Father, I just didn't think anything about it. I was having fun — drunk so often, out with a fast crowd, carousing around. I did just what I wanted to do. Naturally I had no conscience. I didn't believe in God; as a matter of fact, I was a protagonist of atheism.'

"In his riotous living, there naturally came periods of despondency. One night he tried to end everything. He walked along the darkened streets of New Orleans with the conclusion that it was silly to struggle through days and nights of misery, when one stroke could destroy the mechanism which was Von Hertzberg.

"On the Picayune Pier he found a middle-aged man peering into the inky waters. Always able to shift into a sympathetic gear, he questioned the would-be suicide and became greatly concerned with his story. The two discussed the pros and cons of suicide. His logic soon convinced the other man — and himself — that it was foolish to take one's own life.

"The two ended up in a friendly tavern, and both got drunk.

"Years after, he married a charming English girl. The union was a very unhappy one — they were separated just before a son was born. The son never saw his father. While he had no religion whatsoever, his wife's beliefs disturbed him greatly and were the cause of many arguments. Anyway, the fact that his wife's church excluded the idea of the Blessed Virgin was a prominent point in their quarreling.

"This is where Blanche Marie comes in. All that was left in his cynical, blighted soul, was a consuming admiration for the beauty of virginity and motherhood. By nature poetical, he began to frame his verses around the vagary called Pure White Marie. There are dozens of these verses which reflect the man's efforts to combine in one person the only real beauty he seemed able to understand.

"He started to read every book he could find on the Blessed Virgin Mary.

"During this period of argument with his wife, he began to say the rosary every day in honor of Blanche Marie, the pure white one. He still wasn't convinced of the existence of God or that Mary was the Mother of God. It was attributed to her in sacred history and tradition, however, that she possessed the virtues of virginity and motherhood, the highest ideal which he could imagine in any human being.

"He continued to visit the churches in New Orleans just to gaze at the statues of the Blessed Mother. I think in one church particularly, St. Theresa's, he would strike off verse after verse in his confused pagan way.

"Closer and closer he came to a conclusion as he looked at the statues. One day he wrote a poem of thanksgiving, a poem which is my favorite. It is a surprising transition point in his progress toward God. In his tiny handwriting, he wrote:

Should I not ever, Blanche-Marie
　Behold thee with my body's eyes;
　Ay, should I not in any wise
Thy beauty's radiant whiteness see,
Or hear thy voice's melody
　That's lent our earth by Paradise,
　Or win for these my lips the prize
Of putting in the palm of thee
　My heart's whole homage with a kiss;

I still must very thankful be,
　Must have my thanks most fervent rise
To God, and Mary too, for
This: They have given unto me
　The blest belief that 'neath the skies
　There lives thyself in naught amiss.

Should I not ever, Blanche-Marie,
　Behold thee with my body's eyes,
　I must be thankful still — for this.

"Writing poems at a furious pace brought him to another step. Suddenly he capitulated, as he said, to Mary. He appeared at the Jesuit church, just one year after this happy encirclement by the Virgin Queen, and asked for admission into the church. He told the priest:

"'I would gladly take instructions but I don't think it

is necessary. I understand the teachings of the church
because I have done a great deal of reading on those
teachings. Not until now, however, have I believed. I
want to be baptized.'

"He made a profession of faith and received his First
Communion in about 1911. At his shoulder, no doubt,
stood his Blanche Marie, whom he had found at last.

"About this time he quit the *Times Democrat* and
headed for the East, where he worked for a while on the
*New York World*. Before he left, he tried to adjust his
difficulties with his wife. However, he never told me
much about this."

I interrupted the priest's narrative to remark that
Gilbert Chesterton was influenced by the Blessed Virgin
in a similar way. He frequently had drawn sketches of
her on paper, and especially in his great heart. These
tributes to her before his conversion are among the best in
literature. Still he fought off an unseen pressure until he
stood beneath a picture of her in an Italian city.

The priest lit a cigar, leaned back, and came up with
further memories.

"Hertzberg became a dedicated man, like a medieval
champion, for the Virgin Mary. He went to Mass every
day to receive Communion. It seemed a miracle of grace
to friends who had known the old *bon vivant,* to see him
kneeling in childlike simplicity before the altar. When
he was in his room his pen was always busy, mostly about
her who had made him her prisoner of grace. He wrote
thousands of two-line verses in doggerel during these
days.

"They were really prayers in rhyme, which he never

intended anyone to see. They were his expression of his utter dependence on the Blessed Virgin especially during days of grave despondency, which he had even after his conversion.

"After a brief stay in New York, he became a drifter. *The New York World, The Chicago Interocean, The Herald Examiner,* a Catholic paper in the Philippines, and *The New World* received his contributions. He even tried a paper of his own, *The Sunday Estate,* which, like all of his material pursuits, failed. Von Hertzberg's entrance into the church evidently offered no guarantee for even the necessities of good living. He confessed in his roguish way that all of his dreams failed to materialize — all but one.

" 'Father, since I became a Catholic I never experienced so much suffering, poverty, sickness, hardship; but, believe it or not, I have never been so happy. When I am blue I sit down and write about the Virgin Mary.'

"I used to visit with him in his cluttered up room. It was covered with books, papers, and magazines. He smoked incessantly. I often watched him take out a package of Home Run cigarettes and unravel the inner-lining and begin to write on it — he was very careful about spending money for paper. As he propped the lining on a small corner of his desk, and bent over his composition, he was the picture of a grand old philosopher.

"I fell heir to his twenty copybooks of poems and his unfinished assorted manuscripts. Every fraction of an inch of the paper is filled with his minute handwriting. Almost every verse has a title and no two verses are exactly alike.

Each had a line around it to separate it from its neighbor. Each page looks like a paisley design, in black, blue, and gray ink — or like a tightly printed road map, marked with veinlike highways and paths.

"I suppose you are wondering about his boy in New Orleans. The father never got around to visiting him. The break with his family was complete. As Von Hertzberg reviewed his life, he blamed no one but himself for the temperamental difficulties which led to his separation from his family.

"One day he sat in what later was your *New World* office, talking to the editor, Father Donovan, who had just given him a few dollars for a book review — he was grateful for even carfare. This time his carfare happened to be the last he would ever use. The old bard died on the streetcar on his way back to his rooming house.

"In a letter from his son, I learned about the hope of a reconciliation and other news which would have delighted the old man. I'll read you the boy's letter:

Father, as I informed you by telegram, kindly bury my father. I have just finished the 8th grade, and for my graduation gift my mother promised me I could have anything I wanted. I asked for a trip to Chicago to see my Dad. He didn't know I was coming, nor did he know that I have taken instructions and I have made my First Holy Communion. I wanted to surprise my Dad. . . . I look like my father. I would like to have my father's rosary and prayer book.

"The letter was signed, Edward Von Hertzberg.

We who listened were silent, filled perhaps with the inevitable awe we mortals feel in the wake of that unseen force which directs the campaigns of God on earth; no set pattern, no telegraphed design, maybe the smile of a Lady over a truant Knight and his song.

The priest, a little wide-eyed himself, picked up the scattered sheets and handed them to me. He was a sentimental man.

"Take good care of these. I like to think of Von Hertzberg as 'Our Lady's Doodler.' I think he was a saint."

I left with the odd collection of papers and photographs. H.R.R.H. was no longer only an initial, but a reality. He was the man who wandered about the Near North Side like a medieval troubadour, years before of course; but his spirit still walks the streets no doubt absorbed in his Blanche Marie. She never leaves the place where men have sung to her.

# Friar Tuck

IRWIN ST. JOHN TUCKER, the journalist who helped
the priest fill in the portrait of the old vagrant minstrel
Von Hertzberg, was a minstrel himself. The early back-
grounds of these two bore striking resemblances. Both
had begun their newspaper careers in New Orleans. Both
had been and remained Southern gentlemen. Both had
fallen into an ambuscade along the Marian way.

The paths of Irwin Tucker and mine had often crossed when he was religion editor of the *Chicago American*. I had later known him as the Episcopal clergyman who had become pastor of St. Stephen's, just five blocks from my own rectory.

Not until that night when he contributed to the history of Von Hertzberg, did I realize the stature of the man. He had resigned from his ministry just two months before to become a Roman Catholic. The ceremony had taken place in the Franciscan Retreat House at Hinsdale, Mayslake, Illinois, on November 28, 1954. He was nearly 70 now, with the carriage of a man who had made a desperate decision and was supremely happy about it. As he talked to us about Von Hertzberg, I felt I had missed a profound spiritual drama, which had been around me all the while; I was apparently too close to the wings.

He handed me his latest book, *A Minstrel Friar, His Legacy of Song*, with the terse inscription: "To a fellow craftsman." His pen name was Friar Tuck. I glanced at the dust jacket and read the short notice with mounting interest, although I had known something about his accomplishments before. It said that his verses have appeared over a period of forty years in Chicago newspaper columns. Many had been set to music and widely sung. His little Protestant Episcopal church had become a shrine for art and poetry.

I had come to his home with the pastor of St. Margaret Mary to learn more about Von Hertzberg.

Tucker introduced us to his wife, who had just returned from the hospital and looked exceedingly weak. Their three sons entered the room and looked solicitously down at their mother. She was obviously very sick.

I glanced at Tucker, and noted his blue eyes, set generously apart; his strong, long nose; lips, firm and wide across, ready to smile without warning. He reminded me of a kindly, old confessor we had back in my seminary days. He supported his six foot frame on a handsome cane which he had himself made from Ethiopian ebony. He was an expert whittler, and had carved out the history of religion on the cane's surface, from the Old Testament through the New, to the sacrifice of the Mass. We talked about John the Baptist, his patron. Tucker was carving a statue of the Baptist from the leg of an old chest. I thought that the original John might have aged into a benign man like the Friar if he had not been destined to be separated from his shaggy head.

Irwin St. John Tucker was born in Mobile in the Episcopal rectory, where his father had served as rector for many years. In 1887, the sleepy Alabama town was just starting to stretch with a yawn into the modern place it is today. The house was known as "carpenter's Gothic," a type of architecture which is the result of constant additions to a home to take care of the growth of the family. Irwin was the seventh in the procession of ten children. The church still stands he told me, but without its steeple, which succumbed to a sacrilegious hurricane one day and never got back on again. Tucker said:

"That church was the dominant factor in my early years. Through it, and through the rectory, flowed an endless stream of joy and sorrow, of worship and festival, of perplexity and pain. Through the open windows, whenever services were going on in the church, the organ echoed and the murmurous sound of many voices in psalm and prayer filled the great green arches of the live oaks, festooned with moss, that stretched between our home and the House of God.

"That ebbing, flowing tide of worship formed the background of all my early years. The chants and prayers surged and rolled in a wordless diapason around us all, long before I had learned to say the words or sing the hymns."

The relating of God to creation came as naturally to Irwin as the pine scented Alabama air he breathed. His pen became a lute on which to sound the magic of what his young eyes absorbed. His verses were vibrant with the sight of God beyond the horizon. In 1902 he broke out into a rash of composition. He originated a verse form which he called the "crescendo."

He explained that he had created this new verse form to handle the same subject on three different levels. First was the physical; the subject would then extend to the mental; finally to the third level, the spiritual.

As I listened to St. John Tucker (his Baptismal name) and thought of his contemporary, Von Hertzberg, I was struck with the contrast; one nearly bogged down in the physical mire of indulgence; the other, thanks to a solid family background and his physical contact with God's handiwork, accomplished a startling "crescendo" in his life. The third and last level, the spiritual, was more com-

pletely reached by his conversion, so he was even now
cheerfully accepting the fact that he was out of a permanent job for the first time in fifty years.

In his clergyman father's extensive library he busied
himself in the high company of Emerson, Spencer, Milton,
Keats, Shelley, and the English, Greek, and Latin his-
torians; he was consumed with an ambition to become a
great epic poet of America.

His first job after high school was in the freight office
of the Southern Railroad, a job as uninteresting to him
as an empty trunk. Watching our troops return from
Cuba supplied some fuel to his imagination. He wrote
poetry on every available piece of paper, except the railroad record books.

"So, eventually I was fired, to the mutual relief of the
chief clerk and myself."

At sixteen he left Mobile and headed for New Orleans,
a city which enchanted him from the beginning. Its wide
curving streets, the old and the new so quaintly wedded,
the restaurants, the gaiety, the historic haunts, combined
to charm the young romantic.

He lodged with his brother Gardiner, assistant rector
of the Episcopal Cathedral. It was called Christ Church,
the first Protestant church established in New Orleans.
A position with the New Orleans Coffee Co. lasted for
a while. He was fired again. As he gave his explanation
his eyes twinkled with satisfaction:

"The same old reason, a fatal facility for enclosing
poems by mistake for price quotations in business letters.
So I got a job as cub reporter on the old *Picayune*."

He soon became involved in the cross currents of city

and national events. Social and political meetings, police courts, visits of presidents, senators, nobility from Europe, murderers, South American revolutionary refugees. It was a violent change from the serenity of his father's house; but it probably was a fundamental determinant in his life. He was feeling the lift of his "crescendo" without knowing it.

He was discharged from the *Picayune* as a result of a misunderstanding with the editor over a news story. He then joined the staff of the *Item.* The editor had an eye for a good poem and ran a regular column by Tucker entitled, "Editorials in Verse."

Although still a youngster, he was gaining a reputation in the literary circles of New Orleans. A fellow columnist on the *Times-Democrat* met him often in the gay social and intellectual gatherings of the city. It was the elegant and satiric Hans Rudolph Von Hertzberg. Tucker mentioned his name with a degree of enthusiasm. However, he betrayed some sadness as his thoughts skipped back across a half century.

"Hans was unforgettable. In argument he was a fierce antagonist. His pointed mustache seemed to shoot out in fury. With a strong deep voice he would pound out sentences, accompanied by the loud rhythmic thumpings of his cane. At such times a cold bitter blue light would come into his eyes."

Tucker's social conscience was always tender. His daily contact with fires, disaster, industrial accidents, the lack of protective laws for women, the greed and corruption in political quarters smarted him into a new and provocative channel of verse. His column became acutely controversial. He was stretching his muscles in the direction of justice, liberty, and peace and they would never quite relax.

However, he loved the role of troubador more than that of warrior.

Minstrels usually are wanderers. Tucker was true to type. His few years in New Orleans whetted his appetite for travel. After losing his job on the *Item* he moved across Texas to Fort Worth, then to St. Louis for a spell. He finally landed in Chicago, broke and discouraged. He joined up with the old *Interocean* as copy reader. His skimpy pay check paid for a $1.25 a week room on the south side. Tucker was emphatic about his misery in those days.

"Picture me, then, about twenty, in a shabby rooming house, looking out on a very dirty courtyard and alley filled with blackened, rotting snow, while through my desperately homesick memory ran a panorama of the joyous life I had so lately shared."

The copy desk interested him, but the strain on his already weakened eyes was too great. After two years he was forced to go back to Mobile for an indefinite rest. Back in the old rectory he began to improve. His father obtained from the Bishop a lay reader's license which permitted him to conduct services in mission chapels. He was able to establish a chain of small missions in neighboring villages. Gradually young Tucker became absorbed in going farther into the backwoods to instruct people in liturgical worship and common prayer.

The Episcopal Bishop of Alabama would not accept Tucker for the ministry; so he managed to get back on the *Item,* and he promptly wrote for that paper the official carnival poem of 1909, called the "City of Dreams." It seemed to change his luck. Soon after, the Bishop of Louisiana sanctioned his entrance into the theological seminary in New York. He would be ordained in 1913.

Seminary life was a strenuous readjustment for the ex-reporter. Police court and classroom, copy desk and chapel pews, are different enough; but the association with men of apostolic minds, the concentration on doctrine and discipline offered him an entirely new world. As could be expected, he sang about it in rapturous verses, which were viewed with mixed emotions by his superiors. His sturdy approach to doctrine in meter and rhyme was something the theological censors had not contended with before.

He wrote a poem called "God's Wooing," in which he pictured the church as the Spotless Bride of Christ. It was good enough to be accepted by *Harper's Magazine* in 1910. He showed the proof to a professor of dogmatic theology. With puckish humor he describes the scene:

"Well, sir," said the professor, shooting his false teeth out and recapturing them by a dextrous twist of his pendulous lower lip. "Well, sir, at the moment I cannot see anything in them to which I would object."

"My verses did not seem to click any better with him than his false teeth."

As I talked to Tucker, I could see the ferment which possessed the man. I admired the figure of a saint which he had carved from an old chair leg. He showed us pictures of the many wood carvings of Christ, His Mother, and the saints which he had executed for his little church. At the time of my visit he had just completed a wooden plaque of a priest standing at the altar offering the sacrifice of the Mass.

He went back to the first years of his ministry since his ordination in 1913. They were anything but placid. He was assigned to St. Mark's in the Bowery in New York. He found the yoke of Christ sweet and His burden light, but only after he had shouldered a good deal of the load himself. He plunged recklessly into the social unrest of 1913–1914. There were no child labor laws, no workman's compensation. Open warfare existed on the economic front. Labor unions were frowned upon by certain elements. He became an ardent disciple of the socialist Eugene Debs. His zeal for reform in the wobbly standards of society prompted him to conduct a forum under the name of "The Socialist Pulpit" during his first weeks at St. Mark's. Ecclesiastical reaction to it was chilling.

"I went from the seminary with the idea that the proper function of a young priest was to go forth as a kind of Galahad, righting wrongs and challenging evil wherever it appeared.

"It did not take long to discover that this is not the prime requisite of a fledgling in the ministry of the Episcopal Church. What is required is someone to run the Sunday School and young people's societies and to visit uninfluential families."

On a trip West that summer, the young clergyman stopped off in Chicago and accepted the position as associate editor of the *Christian Socialist*, although he still retained his connection as assistant rector at St. Mark's

in New York. But before he went back to his church,
he looked up a little dancer in her studio on Ontario
Street which divides Chicago's 42nd Ward, whom he had
known for seven years. She was Ellen O'Reilly, a practicing Catholic. She was a talented illustrator for the
*Daily Socialist* paper, and also an illustrator of children's
books, which are still used in the schools in Chicago. Her
interest in the young cleric was sincere.

The General Convention of the Episcopal church was
about to be held in New York in that fall of 1913. It
brought hundreds of clergy, bishops, and ministers from
all over the world. The idealistic Tucker expected much
from the discussions. His hopes, however, were shattered
by the dominating influence of two of the convention's
multimillionaires. J. Pierpont Morgan and R. Fulton
Cutting had been the gold plated targets of Tucker's
nationally published attack in *The Living Church*, an
official Episcopal magazine. It was a poem called "Exurgat
Deus" — based on the words by which Moses called for
God to go with his people from slavery: "Arise, oh God,
and let thy enemies be scattered."

Irwin Tucker resigned his post at St. Mark's and again
came to Chicago, in February, 1914. He took over as
managing editor of the *Christian Socialist,* and in July
married Ellen Dorothy O'Reilly.

During World War I, migratory workers and the
unemployed, bread lines and labor problems became
Tucker's special concern. With James Eades How, the
millionaire hobo, Tucker organized the "Hobo College."
It was originally located in the bruised heart of Chicago's
Skid Row on West Madison Street. Later it was moved

to the Near North Side and attracted a colorful assort-
ment of artists and philosophers. They included Jack Mc-
Beth, "The Cosmic Kid," Jack and Jim Sheridan, Jeff
Davis, "King of the Hoboes," Nelson Algren, Ben Hecht,
and Charlie MacArthur. They joined hands, or rather
minds, with the "Dill Pickle Club" which met in an old
barn on Tooker Place behind 876 N. Dearborn Street.
It became a riotous assemblage of rebels in arts and
letters. Jack Jones of the I.W.W.'s, James Larkin, an
Irish revolutionary, Carl Sandburg, with his banjo, Ben
Hecht, Theodore Dreiser, Sherwood Anderson, Austin
O'Malley, John Drury, Ring Lardner, Edgar Lee Masters,
Vachel Lindsay, Manuel Komroff, and Clarence Darrow
rubbed elbows with theater folk, anarchists, budding
authors, and tramps.

Tucker's experiences with the vagabonds from the
College inspired many rugged poems which he told me
"shocked the good people of the fashionable churches
where I occasionally assisted."

His free swinging style encountered opposition. While
on a lecture tour, the *Christian Socialist* fired him by wire.
Always able to bounce back in a hurry he became literature director in the national office of the Socialist party.
His revolutionary pamphlets were read by millions, especially the ones in which he protested against the treatment of conscientious objectors. He was indicted with
five other Socialists on the charge of conspiring to obstruct
the draft. Judge Landis sentenced them to 20 years in
prison. He was in Great Falls, Montana, lecturing with
Lincoln Steffens, when he learned that the decision had
been reversed by the Supreme Court.

His family was growing. He had to get a job. Printer's ink still ran, sometimes riotously, in his veins. He secured work as copy reader on the *Herald Examiner*. The man, with a national reputation in letters, now sat at a work desk with his eye peeled for misplaced commas and split infinitives.

His association with the *Chicago Herald Examiner* and later as the religion editor of the *Herald American*, brought Friar Tuck, as he signed himself, into my newspaper life. The many religious events which we had to feature in the *New World* were also covered by him.

In 1927, he was assigned to the pastorate of St. Stephen's, one of the smallest Episcopal churches in Chicago. The church was practically falling down and had almost no congregation. Tucker whittled away and carved away and succeeded in making the little shrine a place of beauty and devotion. He named it after a poem: "The Little Church at the End of the Road."

Although his devotion to the Virgin Mary was intense in his young days, he later spoke from the pulpit against undue emphasis in her direction. When publicity about the Marian year tribute in Soldier's Field was at its height, he spoke against it in his sermons. With some awe, he told me of his feelings on the subject.

"These honors paid the Mother of Jesus, I thought, were extravagant. I preached against it, as I had often spoken against the invocation of saints, indulgences, infallibility of the pope, and the rosary."

Still he made his way to the field on that September night.

"I went," he said. "Divided in my mind. As a newspaperman most of my life, it appealed to me as an event of importance. I had covered many like it before. Still I had been outspoken against Mariology. I asked myself — What am I doing here? But once I was close to the field my reluctance was replaced by a strong attraction, as if some force were drawing me in."

Friar Tuck interrupted his narrative and looked in at his wife. The little dancing artist lay on her bed desperately ill. We did not know that this would be the last week of her life. She had lingered long enough to see her husband happily secure in her faith.

Tucker returned to the sitting room and resumed his story of the startling developments in Soldier's Field.

"I came toward the statue of Mary, standing white and beautiful, in the glory of the September moon. She wore a robe of white, with mantle of blue. She stood on a crescent moon, with stars in her hair. Something within me cried out: 'Why that's my Mother!'

"As if in answer, a voice sweet and clear like the chiming of silver bells, seemed to say, 'Why don't you come home?'

"My subconscious mind must have raised a protest. An answer seemed to come even more distinctly: 'Child, you are headed the wrong way.'"

Tucker described his great elation as he walked with one of his friends from the field to the subway:

"It was as though I had struggled out of a swamp and found my feet on a firm road. I knew now where I was going and I was on my way."

Irwin St. John Tucker rose from his chair. He had lived longer than most men would have under such tension. His final struggle toward the chapel at Mayslake was a monumental one.

"It felt as if I were on a tight rope which was stretched taut between two opposing forces. It was fraying dangerously to the point of breaking. But when I was accepted into the church I was at peace."

I could almost see in his eyes the reflection of the statue of the "Mother of Jesus, standing on a crescent moon, with stars in her hair. . . ."

# Flicker of a Nail

ST. VERONICA had an early attraction for me. In some verse I wrote for a medical magazine I tried to weigh the contribution which this woman of the Old Testament made in ministering to the Man of the new.

The poem described the courageous action of the First Christian Nurse who wiped the face of Jesus on his fateful journey to Calvary.

> Since then, Veronicas
>     Have stepped from the crowds that shun
> The frightful mask of pain
>     And brought to it the sun
> Of kindness and a rain of solace
>     To its desert of unrest;
> For tangled in the veil

Their charity impressed
They saw their God and His travail.
Across the wounds they dressed
They caught the flicker of a nail.

I was appointed some twenty years later to the pastorate of St. Veronica's in Chicago; and I like to think that a few celestial strings were pulled in heaven by a saint who is scarcely remembered except at the Sixth Station of the Way of the Cross.

The modern woman who devotes her life to the care of the sick has the perfect counterpart in this Palestinian woman, who had a split second graduation into the very essence of nursing. "The flicker of a nail" — the recognition of the kinship between the wounds of man and those of the crucified Christ — could well cause the flame in the heart of a nurse. The cadaver of a hoodlum riddled with shot, or the patient desperately sick with some repulsive disease is hard to associate with the person of One who healed the blind and the halt by the touch of His hand.

But there is no accounting for the spirit in many of the high-minded nurses we know, unless across the wounds they dress they catch the "flicker of a nail."

This recognition is the most beautiful aspect of a profession that has so many facets. It is not always so lovingly practiced as it was on the bitter day of the world's first Good Friday. But seemingly it wells from the heart; and unquestionably it is always rewarded.

I am thinking of a nurse who might have been remotely related to that woman who stepped from the crowd to minister to Christ. Like Veronica, she, too, was Jewish.

Her old-fashioned Hebrew name was shortened to "Rosie." She worked in the emergency room of a hospital close to Maryhouse.

In the old days this room was jumping with emergency calls. The most spectacular of course were the result of the gunmen. Two trigger happy gangs were bent on eliminating each other. Many of them were so successful that places on the street next to the cathedral are pointed out to the owl eyed tourists where several gangsters fell in their tracks. The guide will point also to a second story apartment with obvious delight.

"See that window, folks? From right there, the machine guns blasted the life out of Heimie Weiss and his buddy. Look at the Cathedral cornerstone! It's all spattered with bullet holes."

The gunmen had hired the apartment, propped up their guns and waited for a week before they spied their targets moving along State Street.

And with a final fling at his shaky customers the guide will announce: "You just passed the very center of the gang world. See here below; that's Dion O'Banion's place — O'Banion who was the first victim of the handshake murder."

I suppose no one wondered where these dead and dying men ended their careers. Generally it was in a little room over which Rosie presided with absolute authority. I have seen her perform in these highly dramatic sequences; and I never failed to admire her unshakable mien.

For seven years I attended the hospital from the Holy Name Cathedral. The routine type of sick call was interesting enough. The hospital had the usual background of efficiency, the sterile, hygienically clean corridors under mechanical control. But the place with the red, glowing letters "Emergency" held the very core of drama. It became a field in which the Grace of God flashed about as definitely as the scalpels of the physicians making their incisions on the derelicts, as they lay prone beneath the klieg lights of surgery.

Vaguely I remember explaining to Rosie how important the last sacraments were to Catholics. However, an appeal for her co-operation was not very necessary. She strongly believed in beliefs, and she would certainly bend every effort to see that no dying Catholic slipped through our fingers.

And this nurse, who wheeled material and spiritual salvation into that 15 by 20 room, quite unwittingly became an instrument in the hands of God.

On one occasion, I explained to Rosie the scriptural background of the last rites. I quoted St. James:

"Is anyone among you sick? Let him bring in the priests of the church and let them pray over him, anointing him with oil in the name of the Lord, and the prayer of faith will save the sick man, and the Lord will raise him up, and if he be in sins, they shall be forgiven him."

This promise aroused the professional instincts in Rosie. "Save the sick man" meant in the old Greek "heal." Perhaps in Rosie's mind loomed the prospect of her hospital gaining repute for instant recoveries when all other medical remedies failed. More likely her good heart wanted to co-operate in seeing so many hopeless ones find a better life with their sins forgiven.

How was she to tell whether they were Catholic or not? A medal perhaps, a Hail Mary on their lips, or a rosary in their pockets? Many sort of "looked" Catholic. Would there be a theological cut to their jib which identified them with the bark of Peter?

Rosie was not too fussy when it came to the goodness of God. She exercised her beliefs with amazing energy. There was no stopping her, once she determined that even probable Catholics were going to get the breaks in her little domain.

Many times I would be rung up from the depths of slumber to make my way over to the hospital. Generally the sick calls were bona fide cases: the nurse's eye seemed to have acquired an X-ray quality which could detect a medal or a cross in the most secret of pockets. She had no qualms whatsoever in calling us when an unconscious old fellow would just be mumbling about God. Apparently she felt a soul washing would not hurt even if he had never heard of St. James or extreme unction.

One night a call came in to the Drake Hotel right at the height of a cathedral benefit. A young woman dressed in a formal gown who seemingly had been headed for the event had been struck by a taxi outside the door.

Some ten minutes later I found myself in the emergency room. The patient turned out to be a good Protestant, who in her plight mumbled out some prayers which sounded much like our own. I offered encouragement and a prayer of my own, mostly for patience in explaining to Rosie that it was impossible to cover everyone who prayed.

"Lots of people say prayers," I told her. "Even Hottentots do, I guess. Your zeal is commendable. But there are so many millions in this great city of ours!"

My short instructions sounded perfect — except who knows what God has in mind? And there was Rosie, who never could be cut down into a little, scientific size. You were dealing with her heart and you would be called again when it was not really indicated. "Saving the sick man" was not a phrase to be juggled lightly.

This sacramental service began to gather fame on the other floors of the hospital. The case of the Michigan Avenue jeweler was typical. Two or three heart attacks appeared on his chart. There were times when he held on to life with the determination which defied all medical explanation. He ascribed his many survivals to the sacrament of extreme unction, which by now he had received several times. He was convinced that he had the perfect antidote.

"You know, Father, it does say that the prayers of faith shall save the sick man. So please anoint me again."

It was bewildering enough to see him go back to work time after time. One day when I returned to his old bedside, I asked half in earnest,

"Is this pure and undefiled religion or is it commerce?"

It was worth anything to see him smile, oxygen tent and all.

Not many months ago he came to see me at St. Veronica's rectory in perfect health. I reminded him of my scruple.

"Don't worry about it," he said. "It still must work. I have never doubted the power of God even if I did make him bother about a broken down old shop so often."

As he left, my thoughts glanced back.

Twenty-five years in all with the little things you can't explain. Then to the crooked path toward Calvary . . . Veronica . . . her veil . . . she of the Old law ministering to the New . . . the emergency room . . . and the guide with the megaphone.

"Look where the bullets hit."

Maybe, with more reason: "Look where God struck so often, in so many ways."

## Shower of Roses

THERE were many cases filed in the record cabinet of that exciting hospital near Maryhouse in the middle 1930's. Not all touched on the reign of criminal terror for which Chicago is unjustly celebrated; although it was sometimes difficult to argue that even the Near North Side was surprisingly good, that murder was overplayed by the press, that its grisly details were ladled out for a "who done it" hungry public. The last night-call I answered in this hospital brought me to the bedside of an astonishingly long-lived hoodlum who was now very dead, with the clinical count of 67 shot gun slugs in his body.

As I left the room with the interns and a nurse, I still knew a case like this was the exception. In the ordinary rounds of duty I have seen the silent footsteps of grace stealing into the scene of the sick and the dying. Because they were like whispers from another world and never checked by X rays or instrument, they could not be found on any hospital chart.

I remember particularly a doctor and a nurse who found themselves in the same panel of spiritual influence toward the end. The doctor had had the advantages of strict parental care and tutelage. His father was a skilled surgeon, who died in old age with a splendid reputation. The son died young, with an even greater record of achievement.

The nurse had had professional inspiration too. She was raised by an atheist uncle, a physician, who of course could teach her the techniques of healing of what she felt was the soulless mechanism of the body. When I first met her in my rounds of sick visits, she was an outspoken unbeliever and lived according to her pagan standards. She would shrug off suggestions with a reckless attitude.

"Why bother? What difference does it make anyway?"

The nurse's life was to receive an overwhelming influence from a young woman who died at the age of 24 in the Carmelite convent at Lisieux. Therese of the Child Jesus found her way even into the raucous 42nd Ward.

It is unwise to call every unexplainable phenomenon a miracle. Many remarkable cures are accomplished by science today which years ago would have been labeled miracles. The exceedingly cautious Church demands the most rigorous investigation of any claim to supernatural influence. However, as in the primitive church, there are happenings today which are clearly miracles, such as the cures at Lourdes and the other officially recognized events which we have on record.

A physician occasionally finds himself in the ticklish spot of standing by helplessly while his patient sways precariously between life and death. If he survives, the doctor is given due credit. If the patient, supported by the prayers of the family, by the administration of the priest, manages to pull through, the surgeon might be looked upon as one who probably never should have been called in with his tools. Just how much human skill and divine help are responsible in spectacular recoveries is anyone's guess.

We know there are many ingenious doctors who achieve superhuman results with their patients. We know, too, that the faith in God raised up the dead man at the touch of Peter, and that if one believes strongly enough he can move mountains. Six years in hospital rounds impressed upon me the fact that a great number of doctors rely on God's help in their work. They are more than willing to bow out when they realize that only the great Physician can handle the case.

The devotion of this particular surgeon to the Little Flower was extended to his fellow physicians and the nurses. He was a superb workman in his own right; but he often credited the sensational cures to his heavenly assistant.

I recall him and the skeptical nurse as I read of the 30th anniversary of the canonization of Therese of Lisieux. The world first took notice of the obscure nun soon after her death in 1897. She was destined to live a short time on earth and spend a long while in fulfilling the promise which she made during her last illness. She declared with a naïveté which only could come from a childish heart in perfect union with her Creator: "God will have to do whatever I want in heaven because I have never followed my own will on earth. I believe that my mission is about to begin . . . if my wishes are granted my heaven will be spent on earth until the end of the world . . . I want to spend my heaven doing good on earth . . . I shall not be able to rest, so long as there are souls to be saved: but when the angel says: 'Time is no more,' I shall rest and be happy, for the tale of the chosen will be complete . . . I shall let down a shower of roses to the earth."

This proved to be no idle boast from a misguided visionary. Seven volumes are filled with accounts of Therese's help, healing, guidance, conversions. The soldiers in World War I swore by her, as if she were physically present in the dugouts and with them as they went "over the top." She became their constant companion and a protectress of great beauty and strength.

I remember well one night, when a baby boy was dying with an acute ulceration on the lung. An X ray indicated a last ditch operation in the morning. The frantic mother asked for a relic of the Little Flower, which had been given to us by the Saint's sister, who still lived in Lisieux. All through the night the mother prayed. In the morning, the child was wheeled into surgery. Something had happened, no fever, no torture in the little body. Another X ray was taken. Not a trace of infection appeared. There were the two pictures: the smiling baby, the bewildered staff.

Twenty years later I hired the same boy for circulation work on the *New World*. His husky frame bent over me as he signed the application blank. He had a thrilling history and I was confounded again as I always am in the presence of these things. It was one of so many remarkable cures which I had witnessed myself. No argument was necessary to convince me of the goodness of God in working through Therese of Lisieux, whom He could hardly refuse to honor in her earth-bound covenant.

When we used to discuss these things we would conclude on the note of gratitude. It is comforting to know that God still works signs and wonders as He did among His prophets and the mighty men in the Apostolic church. There is no point in arguing whether the Creator, who swings the world like a bauble at His wrist, cannot choose to reach down and trouble the normal laws of nature. The rationalizing of skeptics can hardly succeed in constricting Him who made their very intellects.

The doctor's influence on a nurse in his prominent role as advocate for the Little Flower, was just a thin thread in that divine loom which will forever gather the loose ends of people's lives into a final pattern. An all-provident God, who marks every swallow which falls from flight, will not rest the loom until His tapestry is complete.

In the meantime the unbelieving nurse was as deep as ever in her disbelief. She was professionally co-operative, however, and her days took her along on spiritual excursions she hadn't bargained for. She was placed in charge of the Communion sets with the two candles, the linens and the crucifix. I have often seen her slightly puzzled as she watched me enter rooms with the golden pyx and the little Eucharistic Hosts. From room to room she accompanied me, silently carrying the tray, with the candles wafting tiny smoke signals before her eyes. Naturally gay and sophisticated, she would on these occasions draw back into a protective shell, like the Samaritan woman at Jacob's well, who tried to escape the invitation in the eyes of Christ.

One day there was a substitute. The nurses at the desk told me that the doctors had given up hope for the nurse who had been my sick-call assistant. Blood transfusion and every medicine had been tried. She probably wouldn't survive through the night. I believed it as I stepped to her bedside. The gaiety was gone. Her head was swathed in bandages. Her whole system quivered under a consuming flame. Her dark eyes peered up through the slits of gauze, which hid running sores. They had attacked her whole body. Her physicians were at a total loss about the cause of her condition.

"I know I am dying . . . I am . . . not going to make it."

I sat there for a long while. I wondered how to approach the malady of her soul, which was so different from the body, with its well-defined veins, muscles, arteries, and bone.

"Have you ever said a prayer?" I asked weakly, fighting for a start.

"No. You know me. No. I've never said a prayer . . . but maybe I could."

Her blistered lips followed the words of an act of contrition. I knew now that she believed. I fumbled with the relic of the Little Flower and put it in her hand. She knew about the saint by now. She had heard the many remarkable stories about favors from Therese.

"Can I keep it for a while?"

She grimaced with a new and awful pain. Her hands tensed around the little disk. An unearthly struggle seemed to permeate the room. Beads of sweat soaked the cloth around her face. I left the room never expecting to see the girl alive again. It was midafternoon.

I heard next day from her friends and from the doctor who had given her up. For no apparent reason her temperature had dropped down below normal. By the time the supper carts passed by the door, she was sleeping a dreamless sleep.

Within the week, she was on her feet and able to work again. Her record still stands in the files. It will say that no one knew exactly what disease she had and what happened on that final day. I only know that some months later she knelt before the altar at Holy Name Cathedral and swept away her past with an Act of Faith: "I believe in God the Father Almighty, Creator of heaven and earth . . ." I only know that she knelt, morning after morning, at the altar rail and received the same Host which she had often seen on her tray beneath the candles wafting tiny smoke signals before her eyes.

And her name was Rose.

# Ebb and Flow

THE offices and the halls of the Cathedral have always been busy and interesting places. But in the 1930's they were particularly interesting. They seemed to be at the crosscurrents in a movement of human action all its own. The present pastor, Msgr. Patrick Hayes, who succeeded the energetic Msgr. Morrison, continues to manage the various departments of the parish with ability and grace. He sometimes remembers, with a wistful smile, how considerably times have changed since we were both assistants in the parish, some 20 years ago, and watched with wide-eyed wonder the multicolored procession of people which came through the doors.

There were the chronic drifters who came in for economic and spiritual direction. A dollar or two sent them on their way. There was no permanent solution for their inability to fit themselves into the framework of society.

There were the very wealthy, who often times had problems, because the accumulation of money in the purse did not necessarily guarantee contentment in the heart.

There were the highly educated. They would come to learn more or sometimes they would come just to impress the clergymen with their erudition.

There were the poverty-stricken persons who lived from day to day, with help from the church or from state funds. For these the priest would have to make out endless forms for the files of the Illinois Emergency Relief.

There were always the "cadgers," the charlatans who had a genius for wheedling a dollar from the slim purses of the curates.

"Father, I have a sick wife and two children in Baraboo, Wisconsin. I must get there tonight. It is a matter of life and death." There was always this element of distance and dire necessity involved.

One woman had a different technique. She gathered stray children and brought them with her, claiming of course that they were all hers. The appeal of five or six sad-eyed urchins clinging to their supposed mother was hard to resist. As well armed with experience as we were, we would again and again be taken in by variations of this particular ruse.

There were the out and out vagrants who make the rounds of parish houses with the persistency of brush salesmen. No doubt there are hobo conventions held in different parts of the country which concentrate on strategy. Campaign charts are probably laid out by the ancients for the guidance of neophytes in the gentle art of panhandling. You can imagine some grizzled veteran pointing out the soft spots to the delegates, who have decided to shun work for the rest of their lives:

"If you want to be sure of an easy buck, head for a rectory. Ask for the young priest just ordained — not the pastor. Give him one of the patented hard luck stories. They've always worked and will again."

The Cathedral rectory was a target for the graduates of this school of swindlers. From morning until night they straggled through the door and slouched down on two benches which faced a long counter. The young man behind it was also a graduate, but in law. He had done the legal spadework on the foundations of Maryhouse and had a deep interest in its survival. Before it was opened he hit upon the idea of asking the ever-present stragglers to help us clean up the house of hospitality for the dedication day. He gathered about a dozen of them who could still swing a mop and finished up the job in a hurry. And his theory on the utter worthlessness of loafers was exploded somewhat by their refusal to take a penny for their services. The spokesman, a snub-nosed, shifty-eyed individual, waved the money away as if it insulted the finer sensibility of his group.

"We ain't taking no dough for this. The charity place is on the legit. We work for nothin' on kicks like this."

The Cathedral offices and adjoining halls were the official centers for many organizations. There were the study clubs, the Lawyers Guild, the Actors' Guild, the

Legion of Mary, the St. Vincent's DePaul Conference, the Holy Name Society, The Altar and Rosary Sodality, The Convert League, and the Cathedral Open Forum.

The Forum was particularly exciting during the depression days. Several hundred people regularly attended the lectures, which were usually given by outstanding persons in the arts and letters.

Arnold Lunn, the English controversialist and author; Michael Williams, one-time editor of *The Commonweal;* Dorothy Day, a former communist and later editor of the *Catholic Worker;* Baroness de Hueck, the dynamic personality in the interracial Friendship House movement; Jane Andersen, special correspondent for the *London Times,* who covered the Spanish War and was at one time condemned to death by a Loyalist court, all these were provocative speakers which made the open discussions after the lectures something to be remembered. Wild demonstrations of oratory from visiting hecklers spiced up the program. "Bughouse Square" supplied a lot of talent for these sessions of free swinging verbal duels.

"Bughouse Square" a counterpart of London's Hyde Park, occupied a small area between Clark and Dearborn Street on the Near North Side. It was a colorful arena of oratory, polemics, theological bickering, itinerant philosophers, and oftentimes just plain fist fights. One zealot would attract his crowd by swallowing razor blades and light bulbs before his talk. A self-styled prophetess would gather a bug-eyed audience by doing a buck and wing dance as a "come on" for her predictions.

Of course summertime was the height of their season.

In winter months, the Cathedral Open Forum offered a warm gymnasium in which these rhetorical athletes could keep in condition for their more important work. Oftentimes an overlydignified lecturer would be jarred out of his complacency by the sight of some dissenter jumping up in the hall and shouting out declamations in the best tradition of Bughouse Square.

The sick calls which constantly flashed upon the switchboard of the Cathedral often bore the stamp of final tragedy. In these, one could always see the silent hand of the Good Shepherd reaching out continually to His stricken sheep. They were not all black sheep. Many were just hopelessly stranded on the bleak rocks of economic or mental ruin, behind the doors of dingy rooms and small hotels, where only the Shepherd could rescue them.

The reverses in which men find themselves toward the end of their lives make an interesting, although distressing, study. I received a letter one day from a girl who asked the priest to look up her father, whom she hadn't seen in many years. Her request came just in time. No one had been near him for a week. I found him in a room which was a shambles. He could hardly move from his bed. His thin handsome face was pinched in the anguish of his last illness. His long silvery hair lay against a dirty pillow case. As he saw me his eyes brightened. He was happy to see anyone, especially the priest. His parched tongue trembled as it held the Blessed Eucharist. He smiled contentedly and relaxed in the bed.

After his funeral, his timid young daughter came into the rectory to talk things over.

"He just disappeared, Father. For years he was president and chairman of a large banking firm. He was hit hard by losses and personal tragedy. I wanted to become a nun, but left the novitiate in order to get a job. He would have starved to death otherwise. Then he wandered off into the unknown. Someone mentioned seeing him on Skid Row. He was sinking lower and lower."

The frail girl trembled a little. She wept softly as she stared across the room. She was seeing again the violent picture of her father's fall from success to failure. She was deep in that bewilderment of mind which seems to struggle to disbelieve it all.

"Finally a friend wrote that he had discovered him in a broken-down hotel. He was very sick and very much alone. I made desperate efforts to get him help. I guess I was too late, wasn't I?"

She thought for a moment. She looked up with an answer to her question poised in her eyes. They were clear now and convinced.

"Maybe I wasn't too late. . . . When he was on top he was — well, I don't like to go into that. . . . Now he is safe. Nothing can harm him any more."

She rose from the chair to say good-by. She smiled a little.

"Really I'm grateful," she said. "It wasn't easy to search all these years to find all this finally. There was no pot of gold at the end of this rainbow's search . . . or maybe there was, when you think of it."

She touched the Bible which lay on the desk.

"I think there is something in there about 'What does

it profit a man if he gain the whole world and suffer the loss of his soul?' "

She paused as if thinking back on many things.

"Dad didn't have two cents when he died, and his wealth and his brilliance didn't help him. But he was rich at the end, wasn't he?"

She left without waiting for an answer. I never heard how she got along or where she went; but I felt that a lot had been answered for her in her short life.

## "... Through Rose-Colored Glasses"

CLOSE to the hotel in which the banker had died there is an old lodging house in the 500 block on North Clark street. From it, on a hot night in July of 1932, a sick call came in to the Cathedral. The priest made his way to the dilapidated house and up the stairs to the bedside of a dying man in a dismal little room. As he administered the last Sacraments, he watched the stricken eyes soften with relief, as if they no longer saw the specter of a tragic past.

The man lay there in utter poverty, with a personal fortune just beyond his reach. All he had left were the memory of a tune and the comfort of the only One who could steady him in the final refrain of death. He was Tommy Malie, the well-known song writer.

The post-mortem articles in the newspapers pointed out startling contrasts in his life. These news clippings on my desk always speed me back, over the twenty some years, to that July night when the distressing sequels in this man's short career were revealed to us. Two items from the *Chicago Tribune* tell the story.

"Tommy Malie, armless composer of popular song lyrics was saved from a pauper's grave yesterday by the intervention of the Society of Authors, Composers, and Publishers, of which he was a member. Funeral services will be held today [August 3, 1932] at St. Vincent's Catholic Church, Webster and Sheffield Avenues, with burial in Calvary cemetery.

"Malie, who was said to have made more than $100,000 on his songs, died penniless, Monday, of alcoholism. Friends said he had squandered his earnings in cabarets and speak-easies. Among the better known of his song hits were "I'm Looking at the World Through Rose Colored Glasses," "Stars Are the Windows of Heaven," "Jealous," and "Highways Are Happy Ways."

Later it was reported in the *Chicago Tribune* that Malie left an estate of another $100,000, which he had earned in royalties, but which he apparently could not collect because they allegedly were withheld by song publishing companies.

It would not be pleasant to consider the story of the uphill struggles of a man, who evidently drank bitter dregs of sorrow from his early years, if its ending was not that of a success story, in as much as he gained the final grace of a happy death.

However, there was only short-lived success in Tommy Malie's thirty-five years on earth. When he was two years old he was run over by a train and lost both arms. He overcame his handicap, and in his early twenties began to make a place for himself among the musically famous of our time. For years he sang on a number of Chicago radio stations, teaming up for a part of that time with "Little Jack" Little. He appeared frequently in the large theaters in the country, but most frequently at the Oriental in Chicago when Paul Ash was conductor of the musical programs.

Malie's appearance, singing his own compositions, was always a treat for his many audiences and when he sang his favorite "I'm Looking at the World Through Rose Colored Glasses," he fairly exuded optimism and rollicking good will.

In 1927, at the age of thirty, he was writing songs which were hits all over the world. In the early 1930's he began to slip into the lazy rhythm of cheap cafés and night life. A $100,000 he had already got on his compositions was soon kicked down the gutters of dissipation. As he sat lonely and alone, in his dingy room in the lodging house on North Clark Street, he hoped in vain for a visit from the scores of friends who had been only too happy to sail with him on his fair weather cruise through money and fame.

And then that hot night in July and the call to his room, where poverty and broken health hovered over him like a fetid cloud. His faith was still strong and he was overjoyed to see the priest in his final hours. As Father Hayes approached the bedside, with his hand raised in benediction, there settled over the room that mysterious calm which comes with God's forgiveness of man.

As the priest held up the Sacred Host and pronounced the words — "Behold the Lamb of God, Behold Him Who taketh away the sins of the world," Malie moved his armless body as if to reach out for the healing Bread of the Sacrament; and it seemed that at least he had gained a fortune at the end; perhaps in recompense for the terrible sufferings of his later years, and his living cheerfully through the physical frustrations of his early life.

His eyes and lips closed as he felt the touch of the holy oils. Somewhere from a distant corner of his mind there could have come the broken strains of the song which had brought him fame, and the words: . . . "everything is rosy now."

Now, at the last, he could be sure of it.

# The Golden Glow

I OFTEN walk the Near North Side in reverie. Each footstep seems to tap out a memory on the mosaic of these streets. Most pieces fit, others never will; but as I think of it the place is solid to my feet despite the fantastic pattern, the violent contrasts of it all.

It was not laden only with derelicts and vice. It had, as it now has, the miracle mile, a graceful avenue of fashion shops, bookstores, art studios, beauty salons, restaurants, and a university or two.

It had the Gold Coast — another mile-long stretch of exquisite apartment buildings and hotels along the lake front. The men and women dwelling on this magic coast had affluence and charm. Their kitchens were filled with exotic foods, their cellars stocked with the finest wines. And they were always willing, it seemed, to invite a hungry young priest in for a steak.

Not many steps to the west the pantries were still so empty, where the stab of poverty somehow reached out to you to jab your conscience some; and you felt guilty about having just finished a *filet* with all the mushrooms stacked around. . . .

Then the tenement on Chicago Avenue . . . The second floor seems quiet now. There are no traces of tragedy any more, such as happened on the summer day fifteen years ago when the wretched man plunged to the street leaving his wife fatally knifed. She had time between her sobs to receive the last sacraments, I remember; and we brought her baby boy to St. Vincent's Asylum.

He smiled a black-eyed, little oriental smile. Where is he now? Full grown I suspect. He would, we hoped, never know about that second floor or how his little heart first faced the world.

Wells Street . . . It always seems to be the second floor. . . . The young mother calling for the priest. She with several college degrees, lashing about in agony, locked finally in the prison of drug addiction.

Over by the river the old deserted tenements where the girl came from late at night to ring our bell. . . .

"Somebody wants to see you, Father," she said. "She's one of my friends. She's awful sick."

The police had urged us to ask for an escort on these late hour calls. Penetrating into the precincts by the river could be dangerous, especially in the days when law and disorder were at shotgun point.

But I didn't call for a squad car that night. It never seemed dangerous with your silent Bodyguard against your chest in the little gold pyx. He trod the streets of Jerusalem while His enemies lay in wait. He entered without a tremor into the circle of sinners who yearned for His merciful touch.

Up four flights of stairs and into the room we went. Startled into silence, I gazed at the woman in the bed. She was as forlorn and abandoned as was the old building, except for the group of her younger underworld friends.

More in question than in command, I managed to say, "Let's kneel down and pray for her."

They knelt in various awkward ways. In a moment the agonies would cease. The grace of the sacrament would take effect.

"May the Body of Our Lord Jesus Christ keep your soul for life everlasting . . ."

I fumbled my way down into the street. Strange emotions came and went — as though I had stood next to Christ that day, when the woman in sin cringed before the murderous mob, and she stretched out her hand to Him in gratitude.

Suddenly I was frightfully alone. He was back there where He was so often accustomed to be, among the fallen ones: "I came not to call the just, but sinners."

I remember on my way home, toward the dawn, nearing the misty shimmer of the waterfront.

There under the bridge, the fires still burned as they did all through those winters of despair. Men and women huddling against the flames, the sparks crackling up, like struggles of hope, and sputtering down again to the greasy cobblestones.

This memory brings me with a start to the fire six blocks north. That, too, was a second floor. All through the day and into the night it burned. Eleven firemen were buried beneath fire and steam. Amid their groans, we brought them the solace of the sacraments.

I swing back in memory to the shelter of the Cathedral house. . . . I remember how happy I was that I lived on the fifth floor high above the houses to the east. From my bed I could always see the turrets of the water tower, washed in a golden light, as if the great Chicago fire has left a blush on its stony face. It never failed to soothe me as the tattered skein of another day unraveled once again.

It was not by accident that I always wanted one final look before my lids flickered into sleep. The question "What's wrong with the world?" was not quite as unfathomable in the glow out there — like the glow in the heart of the living Christ.

At these times I would often think of Gilbert Chesterton, whose answer to the question covered an entire book. He looked at a light like that and saw "the crimson seas of the sunset, like a bursting out of some sacred blood, as if the heart of the world had broken."

Chesterton, the rumpled giant, with his battered hat and flowing cape, had hunched into the room downstairs to say hello on his first visit to Chicago. He hadn't seen the fires beneath the bridge, but he had seen the fierce burning in the souls of men.

In my mind's eyes, the golden aura dwindles, as fog billows in from the lake. I think of the little girl who lay in Henrotin Hospital, close by. I see her vividly now, and can hear her voice. The nurses are hushed, her parents bent in grief. Her body, eight years of lovely growth, is blackened from disease. She waits as I light the candles and take out the tiny Host.

She alone can smile.

"Father, little Jesus will save me."

The glow seems to be gone, as the night mists rally in momentary triumph.

But it is always there.

# The Verdict

THE cat lay tensed. Bewhiskered wastrel that he was, he seemed to feel a gallows chill as he poised for the verdict on his miscreance.

Twilight crept across my reverie. I could dimly see his shaggy head, scarred from his many alley brawls. Suddenly the rumpled fur took on a softer light. . . . He was not at all like the bleary-eyed old ogre of yesterday.

I began to remember how he always landed on his feet, like so many people I had known; they with their mistakes, he with his. It was so important to forgive.

I tugged at the carton of milk. It geysered over my newest suit. I reeled back as if driven by a fire hose.

"*Per aspera ad astra* . . . God help me."
I bent over and gently poured some milk into his pan.
I guess I understood.
He did, I'm sure.